This book is dedicated to the teachers and heads of
St Hugh's RC Primary School in Trafford and of
Beech Hill Primary School in Wigan.
We also thank the children, parents, governors and lunchtime
organisers who got involved.

# Thanks and appreciation

Many of the ideas and activities of Values and Visions draw on the inspirational work of World Studies over the past two decades and we are, in particular, indebted to Robin Richardson, Dave Hicks and Miriam Steiner for their pioneering work.

We owe thanks to those who took part in the Justice, Peace and Integrity of Creation process through the 1980s and who carry that forward now. We are particularly indebted to The World Council of Churches and to the 1989 Basel Conference for its radical call for metanoia.

The staff and children of St Hugh's Roman Catholic Primary School, Timperley and of Beech Hill Primary School, Wigan have contributed vastly. It is the teachers' work with children that largely forms this book. Their commitment to young people and their vision in hard times have provided the bedrock. We thank also the countless teachers who, for years, have daily dedicated their lives to helping children to be truly who they are.

The development group of Values and Visions nurtured the project and formed the community out of which the work grew. Their involvement and contributions have been central. They are: Emma Beresford, Andrew Burns, Sally Burns, Peter Coulson, Geoffrey Court, Jane Dowell, Marjorie Drake, Seamus Farrell, Ann Gill, Alison Hardwick, David Harris, Fazlun Khalid, Steve Miller, John Roussel, Calla Thompson, Veronica Voiels, Pat Waterfall, Anne Yarwood.

For advice, support and inspiration we thank: Jan Ainsworth, Maurice Brunner, Douglas Charing, Meg Chignell, Dave Cooke, Angela Cunningham, Brian Davies, Nora Davies, Suzanne Garnett, John Hammond, Christine Howard, Ben Humphries, Dave Kitchen, Clive Lawton, Tom Leimdorfer, Robin Minney, Martin Palmer, Margaret Regan, Therese Regan, Trish Sandbach.

For written contributions and advice on specific activities we thank: Andrew Burns, Peter Coulson, Geoffrey Court, Karen Davis, Jane Dowell, Fazlan Khalid, Steve Miller, Tony Rae, John Roussel, Roop Singh, Barbara Vellacott, Veronica Voiels, Siri Wigdell.

We thank members of faith communities for their support and wisdom.

We thank all the funders and those individuals who donated money (some of whom wish to remain anonymous), without whose generosity we would have been unable to do this work: CAFOD, The Christendom Trust, Christian Aid, The Christian Peace Education Fund, The Gordon Cook Foundation, The Calouste Gulbenkian Foundation, The Network Foundation, The Joseph Rowntree Charitable Trust, Saint Luke's College Foundation, The United Reform Church, The World Council of Churches.

We thank the staff and volunteers at Manchester Development Education Project: Jane Angel, Steve Bunyan, Lynne Connolly, Dave Cooke, Bob Dinn, David Harris, Cathy Midwinter, Linnea Renton, Anne Strachan.

This work may not necessarily represent the views of any of the above but Values and Visions has grown thanks to them, their support and inspiration.

This book draws on the research and experience of the Values and Visions project, conceived and led by Georgeanne Lamont, 1990-1994.

# Contents

Introduction                                              xi

The Learning Cycle                                        xvi

How to use Values and Visions                             xvii

## PART I: Key Areas of Experience

Encouraging a sense of SELF                               3

Activity 1:   Positive profiles                           5

Activity 2:   Affirmation initials                        6

Activity 3:   Silhouettes                                 8

Activity 4:   IALAC                                       10

Activity 5:   Personal diaries                            12

Activity 6:   Feelings                                    13

Activity 7:   Peer reviews                                15

Activity 8:   Mental maps                                 17

Activity 9:   Mobile maps                                 18

Activity 10:  Our bodies                                  19

Creating a sense of COMMUNITY
in the classroom and school                               21

Activity 1:   Circle time for children                    23

Activity 2:   Guided fantasy                              25

Activity 3:   Today's world is...                         28

Activity 4:   Which community?                            31

Activity 5:   A day in school                             33

Activity 6:   Living the day                              35

Activity 7:   Advocacy                                    37

Valuing the EARTH                                         39

Activity 1:   Heartbeat of a tree                         41

Activity 2:   Trust walk                                  43

Activity 3:   Sounds                                      44

Activity 4:   Micro-hike                                  45

Activity 5:   Dance and music                             46

Activity 6:   Dance and mime                              47

Activity 7:   Webbing                                     48

Activity 8:   The banyan tree                             49

Activity 9:   Earth windows                               51

Activity 10:  Little earth walk                           52

Activity 11:  The banks of the river                      53

Developing openness to SUFFERING
and JOY                                                   57

Activity 1:   Thinking back to a time                     59

Activity 2:   The leaf                                    60

Activity 3:   Meditation on an image                      63

Activity 4:   The beautiful palace                        64

Activity 5:   Alemitu's story                             66

Activity 6:   Caged bird                                  69

Activity 7:   News from Pallem                            71

Activity 8:   100 blessings                               75

Activity 9:   One thing I've enjoyed                      76

## PART II: Key Ways of Reflection

Developing an awareness of ENCOUNTER   79

Activity 1:   Structured interview                        81

Activity 2:   The hoop                                    83

Activity 3:   Rafa Rafa                                   85

Activity 4:   Parents' evening                            87

Activity 5:   Conflict tableaux                           90

Activity 6:   Newcomers                                   91

Activity 7:   The coffee quiz                             92

Activity 8:   The coffee chain game                       94

Enabling LISTENING in the classroom
and school                                                97

Activity 1:   Magic microphone                            99

Activity 2:   Creative listening                          100

Activity 3:   Three tokens                                102

Activity 4:   Active listening                            103

Activity 5:   Valuing a vision                            106

Activity 6:   Listening to the South                      108

Activity 7:   Magic spot                                  110

Developing our understanding and
use of STORY                                              113

Activity 1:   Heroes                                      115

Activity 2:   Raven and the Sun                           117

Activity 3:   Parables                                    120

Activity 4:   Interview as story                          121

Activity 5:   Life stories                                123

Activity 6:   Telling it as it is                         124

Activity 7:   What did they do?                           125

# Contents (continued)

STILLNESS and CONTEMPLATION 129

Activity 1: A time and a place 131

Activity 2: Body and breath 132

Activity 3: Work within the world 134

Activity 4: Journals 135

Activity 5: Staff review 136


Developing SENSORY AWARENESS 137

Activity 1: Mirrors 139

Activity 2: Trust dance 140

Activity 3: Potatoes 141

Activity 4: Two hands on clay 142

Activity 5: Simple hand massage 143

Activity 6: Picture a smell 145

Activity 7: A time to listen 146

Activity 8: Music improvisation 147

Activity 9: The missing ingredient 149

Activity 10: Food for thought 150


Cherishing opportunities for
CELEBRATION and GRIEVING 151

Activity 1: The staff meeting 153

Activity 2: Arriving 155

Activity 3: Welcoming 157

Activity 4: Endings and farewells 158

Activity 5: Festivals 159

Activity 6: The curriculum 160

Activity 7: Dealing with life and death 162

Activity 8: Developing empathy 164


Using VISIONING 165

Activity 1: Waterfall 167

Activity 2: Travelling into the future 168

Activity 3: Mental maps 170

Activity 4: Visiting a world at peace 172

Activity 5: Timelines 173

Activity 6: Setting goals 175

Activity 7: Down to earth 176

# PART III: Purpose and Action

PURPOSE and ACTION 181

Activity 1: Generating class rules 183

Activity 2: Gathering information 185

Activity 3: Tzedakah 186

Activity 4: Traffic lights 190

Activity 5: Strategising 192

Activity 6: Food is rubbish! 193

Activity 7: Letter from the future 195

# PART IV: Some perspectives on Values and Visions

A Buddhist perspective on
Values and Visions 201

A Christian perspective on
Values and Visions 202

A Hindu perspective on
Values and Visions 204

A Jewish perspective on
Values and Visions 205

A Muslim perspective on
Values and Visions 207

A non-faith perspective on
Values and Visions 209

A Sikh perspective on
Values and Visions 210

A whole school perspective on
Values and Visions 211


NOTES 213


BIBLIOGRAPHY 219


ADDRESSES 227

If you could give your child one gift or quality when she leaves school, what would it be?

. . . . . . . . . . . . . . . . . . . . . . . . . . . . . . . . . . . . . . . . . . . . .

This is what some parents,
governors and teachers said
when asked this question:

Tolerance    Happiness

Love    Sensitivity    Wisdom

Compassion

Respect    Selflessness

Education    Truth    Joy

Hope    Spirit of God    Thoughtfulness

Self Value

Peace of mind

Sense of Self

Honesty

Helping others    Christ

Wonder    Freedom to grow

Being secure    Stability

Thankfulness

Values and Visions is about encouraging
these gifts of the spirit.

# Introducing
# Values and Visions

 *"Our lives are inextricably linked by the common thread of humanity.*

*If we break it, we are all undone."*

*Values and Visions* is a way of working. It encourages spiritual development and global awareness and in the process it helps to create community.

The project is for teachers who want to work from, reflect on, develop and explore their values and visions and those of the children and colleagues with whom they work. It starts with the here and now everyday problems, opportunities and challenges that face teachers and children.

Many teachers are feeling overwhelmed and discouraged by the amount of change that is happening in schools. Much of it seems to disregard the needs of the children, the teachers and the school community.

Looking more widely, we find that we live in an age of social distress, disorder and destruction, in a world where the majority live in poverty and oppression. Schools are not immune. The disorder of the world surfaces in school in many ways and the qualities that are needed to address global problems are the very same qualities required in school.

*Values and Visions* is a practical way both of delivering the curriculum and of focusing on the values of the people in the school. It offers a way of finding, even within the everyday turmoil of our school lives, that 'spirit' which can bring clarity and confidence.

*Values and Visions* encourages the development of the whole person across the whole curriculum. It uses play, imagination, stillness and contemplation alongside reason and analysis. It nurtures us spiritually, morally, culturally, socially, creatively and physically. It promotes both the little and the large changes within us that are the process of growth and transformation.

The project is underpinned by certain assumptions:

◊ People matter. Every child and teacher in the school and every one of us has infinite worth and untold potential.

◊ Interwoven in a human being are body, mind, emotion and spirit.

◊ We grow physically, mentally, emotionally and spiritually through actively relating to ourselves, others, the natural world, and the spirit.

◊ We are each part of a community.

◊ Diversity of thought, experience, culture and life forms is the true wealth of this planet.

## Spiritual development

'Spiritual' is not synonymous with 'religious'. *Values and Visions* seeks to work with the deep sense of 'spirit' that underlies all faith traditions and yet is also part of the experience of those who cannot feel at home in any conventional religious context. Poets, musicians and artists have always worked from this source of inspiration, as have many great figures of modern science from Newton to Einstein. Spirituality is a source of creativity open to us all. It brings that quality of aliveness which sparks inquiry, ideas, observations, insights, empathy, artistic expression, earnest endeavour and playfulness. It opens us to life and to each other.

Spirituality is a thread that runs through our life, bringing hope, compassion, thankfulness, courage, peace and a sense of purpose and meaning to the everyday, while reaching beyond the immediate world of the visible and tangible. It drives us to seek and stay true to values not ruled by material success.

*Values and Visions* draws on the view of 'Third World' theologians:

> *"We live our spirituality in response to the cry for life... Spirituality involves people's resistance to dehumanisation... for in each of us as in the whole human community is the urge to live fully as human beings."* [1]

Each school will define spiritual development for itself. Some head teachers in Trafford saw it as:

> *"a growing awareness or enlightenment about the inner self, the purpose of our being and the world of which we are a part. Spirituality is our insight into the real meaning of life and power to live it."*

Whilst the impetus behind this project is Christian, teachers from other perspectives have shared in its creation. It is hoped that it will be of use to those of all faiths and of none. For although each faith tradition is unique, there is among them common ground which is also shared by many people who do not profess a particular faith. The faiths tell us that every human being and all life on earth has value and meaning; we are part of something greater than what we fully see or understand; life is the sacred and the transcendent is always present; we should treat others as ourselves and live in justice and peace.

The faith traditions are a reservoir of wisdom, insight and vital lessons for a world that is divided, dispirited and hungry. We need all the resources of spirit and imagination we can find if we are to be fully human in a world that has grown disconnected, dull and dry in its materialism.

## Global awareness

> *"We face a cumulative series of interlocking problems which endanger human survival. Together they represent a global crisis."* [2]

World Council of Churches

Global awareness is not an optional concern for far-off people and places. It is as much about our own school and our own lives; how individually and together we are 'world players' with responsibility for the type of world in which we wish to live. Unfair trade, international debt, a world economy quite literally in the arms of war, the relentless pillaging and pollution of nature — these big world issues touch every corner of our lives from what we eat for breakfast to whether our school budget is adequate for our educational needs, or whether the children will find fulfilling jobs when they leave school. They have severe consequences for the poorest everywhere, but especially for the countries of the so-called 'Third World'.

The majority of the people on this planet live in the 'Third World'.[3] The term is taken to mean the many countries in Africa, Asia and Latin America, impoverished by centuries of economic exploitation. But the Third World also exists in the richer countries, for each has its class of impoverished people who do not share the 'First World' — they do not enjoy the same standard of living and their voices are not heard in the decision-making processes of their society; their cultures are often disregarded or destroyed.

> *"The Third World offers values which can only be found with difficulty in other places... community instead of individualism, simplicity instead of opulence, helpfulness instead of selfishness, creativity instead of enforced mimicry, celebration instead of mere enjoyment, an openness to transcendency instead of dull pragmatism."*

Jon Sobrino [4]

This project seeks to explore the differences in resources and power between those in the 'First World' and those in the 'Third' and to listen to the values and visions of people of other cultures as well as those of the West. It recognises that positive steps are being taken, often on a small scale, by people all over the world to care for the diversity of life, change the way things are done, give everyone more of a say in their own future and combat human suffering.

Schools can be part of this. By relating what is happening locally to what is happening globally, by teaching about issues to do with justice, peace and care for the earth, by showing within the life of the school ways of tackling injustice, violence and environmental abuse, we help the children develop within themselves the resources to contribute positively to the world in which they live.

## Community

Schools are a microcosm of the world. As we draw on shared values, accept and learn from our differences, and begin to grasp a sense of our interdependence with all people, community can grow. Genuine community is open and inclusive, valuing and involving all the individuals and groups within it and creating a door to the wider world. Any school can become a community which models how the world may be; for example, a place where each person is respected and honoured, relationships are based on mutuality rather than power and resources are used mindfully and justly.

## Every now and then

Every now and then, one walks into a school which is special. One knows immediately this place is different; there is a hum of activity; people are glad to be there; there is a sense of purpose and well-being; people are relating to one another with confidence and respect; there is an openness, an aliveness and the wider world is there. There are many elements at work in such a school but valuing oneself, others and the earth provides the bedrock. Such schools offer a glimpse of a future world that works for all. *Values and Visions* can support your school in being part of this.

# Values and Visions

## THE LEARNING CYCLE

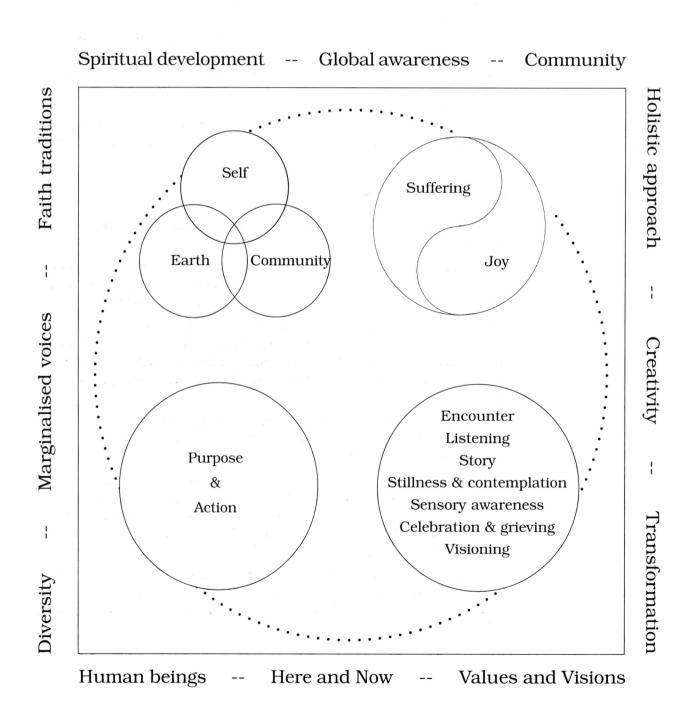

Spiritual development  --  Global awareness  --  Community

Faith traditions

Holistic approach

Marginalised voices  --

Creativity  --

Diversity  --

Transformation

Self

Earth  Community

Suffering

Joy

Purpose
&
Action

Encounter
Listening
Story
Stillness & contemplation
Sensory awareness
Celebration & grieving
Visioning

Human beings  --  Here and Now  --  Values and Visions

# How to use
# Values and Visions

## 1   THE LEARNING CYCLE

The diagram opposite shows the learning cycle which has provided the format for this book.  We start from our own experience which falls into three key areas: self, the community or communities we live in, and the earth.  Our experiences in these areas open us up to suffering and joy.  We then reflect on our experience using one or more of the key ways offered.  This reflection helps us to focus on our purpose ('What do I want to do about..?') and to decide whether, and how, we act.  The action we take gives us new experiences, generates new feelings to reflect upon and so the cycle continues.  The aim of this cycle is transformation: inner change which leads to outer change.

## Key areas of experience

Experience includes all the raw material of life that we have to work with and develop.

*Self* is about my experience of who I am as a unique individual of infinite value and untold potential.  It includes warts and all.  It is about my relationship with others, the community and the earth.

*Community* is about a living, growing, changing group of individuals who share resources, cultures, values, visions, history and endeavours.  It might be the family, friends, class, school, faith group, neighbourhood, country, world.  Its central principle is interdependence.

*Earth* is about our immediate, local, national and global environment.  It is about being part of the web of life and celebrating creation.

*Suffering* and *joy* go together.  Suffering is pain, physical, emotional or mental.  It takes the form of discomfort, anxiety, fear, loss, grief, despair.  It can be about violence or oppression, or the misery of alienation.  It includes the suffering of whole communties through injustice, oppression or environmental destruction.

Joy is about enjoying life in its fullness.  It can involve savouring, delight, gladness, contentment, wonder, happiness, thankfulness, well-being, peace.  It is about a sense that all is well.  It can co-exist with suffering.

## Key ways of reflection

In reflection we respond to, think about and work with our experience.

**Encounter** is about relating openly to others and to the earth.

**Listening** is about giving undivided attention, using our ears, eyes and heart to understand, learn from and communicate with others.

**Story** is about making sense of experience through the telling of it.

**Stillness** and **contemplation** are about taking space and time to make sense of our experience and to be truly present in the here and now.

**Celebration** and **grieving** go together. Celebration is about treating each day as new and special and being glad to see all that is of beauty and value wherever we are. Grieving is a response to our own and others' suffering. It can engulf us but it can also lead to acceptance, action or even celebration of something new in our lives.

**Visioning** is about exploring images to visit the past, present and future. It can be a process of healing or inspiring ourselves.

## Purpose and action

Action embodies what we decide and what we do. It arises from our experience and reflections. In turn, it creates new experience.

**Purpose** and **action** are about living out our values at the immediate, local and global levels. Purpose is the motivation and focus that comes from our values and vision. It gives meaning to our life and that of our community. Action is the follow-through of this. It is about putting our values and visions into practice.

Once we experience our deep interconnection with the world around us, once we grasp the fact that everything we are or do has an effect, we grasp the great importance of what we choose to be or not be, to do or not do. Together purpose and action can be transforming.

## 2   GETTING GOING

### Where do I begin?

There is a section in the book for each of the three stages in the learning cycle: Experience, Reflection and Action. Within each section are activities dealing with the different elements of that stage (self, community, earth, etc).

1   Reflect on your values and visions and decide what really matters to you.

2   Decide what challenge is facing you here and now.

3   Locate that concern in one of the 'Key areas of experience' (Section I).

4   Identify which 'Key ways' (Section II) would be helpful for reflecting on that experience.

5   Select activities from both sections and adapt them according to your values and vision.

6   Work within a group/community so that the wisdom of that community can provide checks and balances.

7   Develop your future action drawing on the values and visions you have articulated for yourselves. Use the activities in 'Action' (Section III) as a springboard for your own ideas.

8   Remind yourselves of the underlying principles of *Values and Visions* (on page xii) and 'Am I doing *Values and Visions?* (on page xxi).

## The activities

The activities are organised with these elements:

### *What are you doing now?*

This identifies curriculum concerns and other issues in school or community life that are explored by the activity.

### *You might like to try*

This gives the instructions for doing the activity. We hope that the majority of the activites are used with both children and adults. However, where an activity has been written with a certain group in mind this is indicated by the boxed C for children, A for adults, C/A for both. Most activities can be adapted for use with either group. An appropriate context needs to be found.

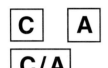

Sometimes there are italicised comments at the bottom of this section which are based on our experience of the activity.

'V&V' appears in all activities in Section 1: Key areas of experience, as it is intended to identify what it is in the activity which makes it *Values and Visions* and not just any other piece of schoolwork.

We have vignettes from teachers and children of their experiences in doing the activity. They are displayed in shadowed boxes.

Quotations from faith traditions and other sources are displayed in the outside column of the pages. They are there as inspiration and food for thought. If you like any of them or if the children like any of them, you may want to reproduce them in your work — as illuminated prayers or meditations on the wall during a particular project or as a short reading before an activity begins, and so on.

# 3  AM I DOING VALUES AND VISIONS?

If, at some point during the week, you find yourself saying "yes" to any one of these questions and if, over a year, you have done something on each of them, then the way you are working is the way others are working in *Values and Visions*.

1  **Human beings:**  Are we treating people as unique individuals who matter?

2  **Values and visions:**  Are we aware of what gives meaning and purpose to our life, our school, our world, and working from the vision we have for them?

3  **Here and now:**  Are we starting with everyday problems, opportunities and challenges that face us as teachers and children and exploring practical activities and strategies that apply to the here and now?

4  **Spiritual development:**  Are we open to the transcendent, acknowledging that there is more to life than meets the eye and making time and space for awe and wonder?  Do our actions lead to justice, peace and care for the earth?

5  **Global awareness:**  Are we acknowledging the oneness of humanity and all life and addressing the challenges that face the planet?

6  **Community:**  Are we creating within school a microcosm of a caring community where individuals and groups are valued, involved and part of the whole; where shared values and visions can include individual perspectives?

7  **Faith traditions:**  Are we drawing on the insights and wisdom of faith traditions?  Does our work have meaning for those of all faiths and those of none?

8  **Marginalised voices:**  Are we recognising that we have much to learn from other cultures, classes and peoples, especially the so-called 'Third World' and the impoverished and oppressed within our midst who make up two-thirds of the world population?

9  **Diversity:**  Are we recognising and valuing our differences as individuals and groups, working towards equality and challenging all forms of prejudice that divide us?

10  **Holistic approach:**  Are we teaching in ways that nurture the whole person — physical, emotional, mental, aesthetic and spiritual — and considering the school as a whole?

11  **Creativity:**  Are we using all our energy and abilities and drawing fully on our natural creative resources?

12  **Transformation:**  Are we creating a school where transformation takes place; where the familiar is seen with new eyes?

# PART I

# Key Areas of
# EXPERIENCE

# Encouraging a sense of
# SELF

"When we deal with that familiar humdrum reality, the world of human beings, it is necessary to remember in some way that we are dealing with extraordinary things, beyond the imagination of science fiction.  This is a fact to which poetry, familiar wisdom and the traditions of nations all attest.  Human beings are creatures who are free, immortal, loved by God; creatures who are historical, who have a past and also a future, who are called to work for a kingdom of love and justice."

*Mandlenkhosi Zwane*
*Bishop of Swaziland*

Self is about:

◊  who I am

◊  my relationship to others, community and the earth

◊  my being a unique individual of great potential and infinite value

◊  my purpose.

Schools are about children. Teachers, when asked what is important to them, have consistently said that it is the children that matter. Teachers have expressed their priority as being to help develop the whole child to fulfil their full potential so that they can contribute to society.[5]

The teachings of faiths support the teachers' view. Be it Islam, Christianity, Judaism, Hinduism, Buddhism, Sikhism or the wisdom of first nations people,[6] the verdict is quite consistent: the human being is a creature of infinite value and great potential called to be something much more than a passer of tests. In Christianity each is seen as a child of God, in Islam as a steward of creation, in Judaism we are called to be involved in co-creating with the Creator. In Sikhism each has a part of the divine. In Hinduism, beneath the passions of human life, our essential soul is infinite, perfect and divine. In Jainism, too, our beginningless, endless self has the potential to unveil its perfection. In Buddhism, our true and unlimited nature embraces, and is embraced by, all beings. In a nutshell, each one of us is a wonder of the world. Be we of any faith or no faith, it might be well to pause before discounting the wisdom of thousands of years lived out in countless lives.

Whether of a faith or of no faith, the question is "how are we to value children?" It is a question of common sense. Few teachers would deny that a child who is confident and has a true sense of self worth is much better able to learn than a child without that sense of worth. And it is not only the children. Each person within the school who feels fully valued is better able to contribute and, moreover, provides a model of what we may be.

In this section we look at a few simple activities that are about playfully developing the sense of self worth in people in the school. The activities are not new. The context may be new: when working on self-esteem we are working on something very fundamental, the basic belief about what a human being is and what they are doing here on the earth.

The activities in this section are about recognising and cherishing not only strengths and qualities, but also feelings, values, perceptions and hopes. It is essential that they are used in the context of valuing each child's (and adult's) race and gender. It is of little use to affirm someone's qualities whilst everything else in the school denies their identity. If a black Muslim girl comes into school and all the stories are about little white boys, if the history is about white men, if the images are of men, if the only faith valued is Christianity (or if no faith is valued), that child's experience of herself finds no reflection in school. Structures and policies on equal opportunities are needed to support the activities.

One of the best ways of affirming someone and supporting their sense of themselves is to share responsibility with them. When children are involved in reflecting, making decisions and taking responsibility they blossom. The individual's sense of self cannot be separated from his or her sense of being part of and valued by the community.

> "The idea expressed in the Biblical 'love thy neighbour as thyself' implies the respect for one's own integrity and uniqueness; love for and understanding of one's own self, cannot be separated from respect and love and understanding for another individual. The love for my own self is inseparably connected with love for any other being."
>
> *Erich Fromm*

# P ositive profiles

ACTIVITY 1

This activity is about sense of self, reflection, celebration, valuing creativity.

## What are you doing now?

◊ You may be working on profiles and records of achievement.

## You might like to try  C 

The required profile and records of achievement for each pupil can be turned into an affirming document.

1 Photographs are taken of the child as she undertakes something new, shows marked improvement or acquires a new skill, and are included with descriptions written by or with the child. The emphasis is on what she can do.

2 Things outside the school that are important to the person are given equal weight to school achievements.

3 The person has regular access to the document so it becomes something she "owns" and is proud of.

> In the course of an informal conversation, three top junior boys timidly told me how they were helping crested newts. They were transferring them, in a bucket, from a polluted pond in the grounds of a nearby cloth-dyeing company to a temporary pond they had made in the backyard of one of the boys' homes. They were looking for a new, clean pond to rehouse the reptiles. They knew all about crested newts and knew, too, that they could be in trouble for being on the company's property or for tampering with an endangered species. Yet without the boys' help the newts would have died.
>
> The school was not aware of the boys' knowledge and skill with the animals. As far as they were concerned the boys were of 'below average ability'.
>
> *Teacher, Bury*

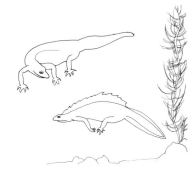

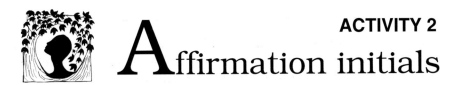

# Affirmation initials

 This activity is about sense of self, creativity and fun, relationship, cultural diversity and story.

## What are you doing now?

◊ You may be taking the register at the beginning of each day.

◊ You may be opening an in-service session.

◊ You may be doing language work on adjectives.

◊ In RE you may be doing work on valuing self.

*"Hold no man insignificant and nothing improbable, for there is no man who hath not his hour and no thing that has not its place."*

*Sayings of the Fathers*

## You might like to try $\boxed{C}$

1 Children work through the alphabet, finding adjectives that can be used to describe people's qualities in a positive way.

2 The adjectives are displayed on posters or recorded in a class book.

3 The children choose two words to describe themselves, one beginning with the first letter of their first name and the other beginning with the first letter of their second name, for example Super Sally Brilliant Burns or Gentle George Laughing Lawrence. The names can be used on badges or posters. They can be made into name plates based on Arabic, Hebrew or Chinese calligraphy. They can be included in a person's profile. They can be the way into a project on names: the history of names; the meaning of names; how you got your name; naming customs in different cultures and many more.

4 Some questions you might like to discuss:

Do you like your 'new' name?

How did it feel to describe yourself in a positive way?

If it was difficult to say good things about yourself, why might this be?

How can we help others to like themselves more?

How can we help each other feel comfortable saying "I like myself"?

莉娜
Lena

*"The most terrifying thing is to accept oneself completely."*

*Carl Jung*

Comment: *The epithets chosen by each person can be very useful in diffusing conflict. When a teacher feels cross with a child, it can help her and the child calm down if she uses his affirming names. Asking adults to introduce themselves using affirmation initials can be a good ice-breaker and a way of creating a positive atmosphere in an in-service session.*

Children were asked in pairs to take a letter of the alphabet each and to find any and all affirming adjectives in their dictionary. They then looked round the class and found people to whom the adjectives applied.

## Positive adjectives to describe people

**A**
able *Cerys*
acceptable *Glyn*
accomplished
active *Kelly*
adept
admirable

**B**
bashful *Glyn*
beautiful *Sian*
best *Jade*
bold *Kenon*
brilliant *Kelly*

**C**
careful *Davon*
caring
cautious *Gwenan*
champion *Kelly*
chatty
clever

**D**
dainty
daring
decorous
delightful
dynamic

**E**
eager
elegant
enterprising
English

**F**
faithful
friendly
funny

**G**
gorgeous
gentle
glad
glamorous
good

**H**
happy
helpful
hilarious

**I**
ideal
idealistic
immaculate
intelligent

**J**
jokey
jolly
just

**K**
keen
kind
kind-hearted
kissable

**L**
law-abiding
lovable
lovely
loving
lucky

**M**
marvellous
merry
mighty
mindful

**N**
nice
noble
notable

**O**
obliging
observant
optimistic
outstanding

**P**
patient
perfect
pleasant
powerful
pretty
proud

**Q**
quaint
quick
quixotic

**R**
realistic
refined
regal
respectable

**S**
saintly
sensational
sunny
super

**T**
terrific
tremendous
trustworthy
truthful

**U**
useful
unusual

**V**
virile
virtuous
vivacious

**W**
warm
welcoming
well
Welsh

**Y**
young

**Z**
zany

Teacher, Wales

ACTIVITY 3
# Silhouettes

 This activity is about sense of self and valuing others; it involves valuing cultural diversity; reflection and the community.

## What are you doing now?

◊ You may be doing language work.

◊ You may be doing RE.

◊ You may be trying to recreate harmony in the classroom after a conflict.

## You might like to try C

"What is a man profited if he shall gain the whole world, and lose his own soul?"

*Matthew 16:26*

You will need a piece of sugar paper, longer than the tallest person in the class, a thick felt pen, a small card for each member of the class (including the teacher).

1  The children sit in a circle.

2  One person lies down on the floor on a large sheet of sugar paper and another person draws around her/him in felt pen.

3  Each child, including the two in the middle, has a small card. On it they write something they like about the person whose silhouette has been drawn.

4  The cards are collected by the person who drew the silhouette and given to the person who was drawn to read out.

5  The silhouette is decorated to look like the person it represents and the cards are stuck on or around it.

6  Over a period of a few days this is done for each person in the class, including the teacher, and the silhouettes are displayed prominently.

Alternatives: if space is a problem, just a hand can be drawn around, or a profile can be made using an overhead projector.

Affirmation Consequences: in small groups each person writes her name at the top of a piece of paper then passes it to the right, with each person writing something positive about the person whose paper she has. This is repeated until everyone gets her own piece back. The papers are read out by their owners.

"The supreme God dwells in all beings equally."

*Bhagavad Gita*

**7** Some questions you might like to discuss after the activity:

How did it feel to have good things said about you?

How does it feel to have bad things said about you?

How does this make you feel about others in your class?

Does it matter who said what about you?

How can we become more comfortable about saying what we like about each other?

If it was difficult to say good things about someone, why might this be?

What can we, as a class, do about this?

Comment: *It helps considerably if affirmation is part of life and not just confined to this activity. It may happen that someone feels they really cannot find anything good to say about the person being affirmed. If this were the case, it would be better to write nothing than to write something negative. It could also be helpful to discuss why the person has this difficulty and what should be done. Having said this, in our experience, the situation has never arisen and we would emphasise that preparation of the group beforehand is essential.*

M atthew got on everyone's nerves. He disrupted every lesson and his peers and his teachers were heartily sick of him. Every form of punishment and sanction had been tried but with little effect. Then we decided on another approach: affirmation. We told the class we were going to do something a little different and wanted a volunteer. As we predicted, Matthew came forward. We affirmed him using affirmation silhouettes. For once in his life, Matthew was speechless. Everyone had found something they liked about him. When he regained his cool, he kept asking "Who wrote this?" "Is it true?" The class assured him it was. It may sound dramatic, but it changed Matthew's life. It changed ours too. I wonder if he still has the cards somewhere...

Teacher, Wales

"Perhaps the most important single cause of a person's success or failure educationally has to do with the question of what he believes about himself."

*AW Combs*

# ACTIVITY 4

# I A L A C

**V&V** This activity is about sense of self, reflection, action, suffering and joy.

## What are you doing now?

◊  You may be taking assembly.

◊  You may be doing work in RE on how we treat others.

## You might like to try $\boxed{\text{C}}$

You need: a poster with the letters I A L A C (I Am Lovable And Capable) written on it; a sticky label for each person in the class/ group.

**1**  Read or enact the following story:

Tamara gets up in the morning.

Tamara: "What a lovely morning. I feel great. I think I'll do my hair in that new style Jill showed me."

Tamara goes downstairs.

Mother: "You're late, and what on earth have you done to your hair!" (Tamara tears off the 'I'.)

Tamara eats her breakfast, collects her school bag and heads for the door. As she's going out she turns and calls out:

Tamara: "Is it OK if I go to Jill's after school? I'll only be an hour. She wants me to listen to her new CD."

Father: "That's right! Anything to avoid helping out at home. Isn't that typical? All you think of is yourself." (Tamara tears off the 'A'.)

Tamara arrives at school, then in class she talks excitedly to her friends about some work she is enjoying. The teacher looks up.

Teacher: "What's all this noise? Have you people no self-control? Didn't I tell you all to get on quietly? You never listen!" (Tamara tears off the 'L'.)

Later, another teacher is handing back some work. She comes to Tamara's.

Teacher: "This is much better than last time; in fact it's a real improvement." (Tamara picks up the 'L'.) "You can't have done it by yourself. Who helped you with it?" (Tamara drops the 'L' and tears off the 'A'.)

"When children know that they are valued, when they truly feel valued in the deepest parts of themselves, then they feel valuable. This knowledge is worth more than any gold."

*M Scott Peck*

Walking home from school with her friends, Tamara remembers the argument at home that morning.

Jill: "Are you coming back with me to listen to my new CD, Tamara?"

Tamara: "I can't. My Dad says I've got to go straight home. Sorry."

Jill: "Go on then, be a Daddy's girl! Come on, everybody. We'll go and have some fun without her." (Tamara tears the 'C' into pieces)

2  Some questions you might like to discuss:

How does Tamara feel at the start/end of the day?

Have any of us ever felt like that?

What was it like?

What can we, as a class/school, do to ensure people feel good about themselves?

3  Each person makes and wears a badge with the letters IALAC on it.

4  Each time something bad is said/happens to them they tear off a letter.

5  Each time something good is said/happens to them they add a little decoration to the badge.

6  In a circle at the end of the day/week, the children share what has happened to their badges.

7  The object is to keep the class badges beautiful and intact, so people/children have to be especially careful with each other.

Comment: *This is a good activity for an assembly and can make affirmation a whole school objective.*

"The secret of education lies in respecting the pupil."

*Ralph Emerson*

**ACTIVITY 5**

# Personal diaries

 This activity is about gaining a sense of self through reflection; it involves story and will touch on suffering and joy.

## What are you doing now?

"The pearl is hid in the field, and the field in the world and the world is in your heart, and there you must dig deep to find it, and when you have digged deep and found it, you must sell all to purchase and redeem this field."

*George Fox*

◊   You may be working on language.

◊   You may be writing your daily/weekly news.

◊   You may be recording what you have done with the class.

## You might like to try

1   Children are encouraged to keep personal diaries and are given time to write in them.  Photographs may be used to illustrate them.

2   If the child wishes, excerpts from the diary may be read out in class.  Otherwise it is kept completely private.

3   The child is encouraged to re-read her diary, periodically.

4   Some questions you might like to discuss:

What do you like about keeping a diary?

What do you not like?

How do you feel when you re-read your diary?

Comment:  *Writing a diary is not just about 'news', it is about feelings, good and bad, about having a safe place to express every part of you.  It is about taking time for reflection.  It helps develop awareness of who you are.  It is not just a writing exercise.  The right to remain private is respected.*

# ACTIVITY 6
# Feelings

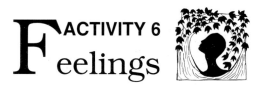

 This activity is about sense of self, community, suffering and joy, listening, values; it may well involve justice, peace and the environment.

## What are you doing now?

◊ You may be reacting to an item of news the children have brought up.

◊ You might be working on RE or language.

## You might like to try C

You will need a sheet of paper and a pen for each person; a large sheet of paper and pen for a class/group poster.

1 Individuals reflect on what makes them feel different things. The feelings are listed as follows (choose some from the list):

> When I see/hear..., I feel happy.
>
> When I see/hear..., I feel sad.
>
> When I see/hear..., I feel hopeful.
>
> When I see/hear..., I feel hopeless.
>
> When I see/hear..., I feel irritated.
>
> When I see/hear..., I feel silly.
>
> When I see/hear..., I feel glad.
>
> When I see/hear..., I feel awful.
>
> When I see/hear..., I feel peaceful.
>
> When I see/hear..., I feel I want to help.

2 In pairs, one listens without comment, while the other spends two minutes talking about her feelings.

3 Swap over.

4 Together look for similarities.

5 In a circle, the pairs feed back the feelings they had in common. These are recorded on a class poster which can include the children's painting or other visual representations of different moods.

"I thank You, Lord, for knowing me better than I know myself, and for letting me know myself better than others know me."

*Father-in-law of Mohammed*

"When you ask me how I feel, I'm the only one who can tell you! And I like that!"

*Kindergarten student*

**6** Some questions you might like to discuss:

Why did you have these different feelings?

How can you support each other through painful feelings and celebrating together joyful feelings?

**7** The class is invited to make a commitment to the support and celebration of feelings in the class. It's all right to have feelings.

Comment: *Boys especially can be made to feel silly when expressing tenderness, and it helps to know that others share the same feelings.*

# P eer reviews    ACTIVITY 7

 This activity is about valuing others; it involves reflection and listening.

## What are you doing now?

◊ You may be completing any individual piece of work.

## You might like to try

1 When a piece of work such as a painting has been completed, individuals get into pairs and swap work.

2 Think of at least three things you like about your partner's piece of work and any one thing you feel your partner could develop further or improve on in the future.

3 One of the pair has a set time (say, one minute) to talk about the work while the other listens and perhaps (depending on age and ability) makes notes. The listeners must listen and not interrupt. They are free to comment when the time is up.

4 Swap over.

5 Some questions you might like to discuss:

How does it feel to have someone talk about your work?

How does it feel to comment on someone else's work?

What does it feel like to listen without comment? (See the section on Listening, page 97.)

What does it feel like to be listened to?

What do you learn from sharing your work with someone else?

"The reason angels can fly is that they take themselves so lightly."

*GK Chesterton*

## Star for the day

A corner of the room was set up with a large mock television screen. Each day, at story time, a child became star for the day. They had prepared for it by bringing in photos or anything about themselves. The class then interviewed them 'on TV' on their likes and dislikes, interests and anything else about their lives. Each day a new child became star for the day. The children became very involved and listened intently. When one child happened to repeat a question his neighbour went, "Ssh - she's already told us about that - weren't you listening?" By the end of the first term the children really knew one another well and as teacher I knew things I would never have found out about otherwise.

*Infant Teacher, Trafford*

It was our first team meeting on the new project, the first time we had sat down together to plan how we would work. The four of us knew each other, but we had never worked so closely before. We were all a little apprehensive. We began the meeting with affirmation consequences. I affirmed my colleagues and suddenly I knew why we had been chosen for the job: we were a great bunch of people and our skills complemented each other wonderfully! However, when we came to read out our cards I realised that one member of the team had written something untrue about another: a quality he wanted her to have, not one she possessed already. That immediately cast doubt on what he had written about me - did he really mean it? I never plucked up the courage to ask him.

*Trainer*

# Mental maps

ACTIVITY 8

 This activity is about values. It involves creativity, justice, peace and the environment, reflection and listening.

## What are you doing now?

◊ You may be preparing an assembly.

◊ You may be reacting to an item of news the children have brought up.

◊ You may be preparing an in-service training session.

## You might like to try  C / A

You will need a sheet of paper and coloured pens for each person.

**1** The class/group is told the following:

"There's this Martian. She has just arrived on Planet Earth, and you are the very first human being she meets. She is friendly and intelligent, but doesn't understand your language. You draw a sketch plan of the planet or your neighbourhood, to show the Martian what is going on at the moment."

**2** Each person then draws his map.

**3** The group brainstorms: things I like about my world... things I don't like about my world...

**4** In a circle, each person then shares: What I think matters most is...

Comment: *This can be used in in-service training to discuss an issue such as sexism. Instead of a map of the planet or neighbourhood, the group is asked to depict a school which is both overtly and subtly sexist. The group discusses how closely this resembles the school(s) they work in.*

**M**obile maps

 This activity is about the person's own story and our interdependence with the local and global community.

## What are you doing now?

◊ In geography you might be doing work on compass points.

◊ In RE you may be working on self and others.

## You might like to try C

You will need a large open space to work in.

**1** The teacher places herself in the centre of the room and states which place she represents, and then asks the children to place themselves relative to her, for example:

> "I am in the school. This is north, (pointing) south, east and west. Place yourselves around me to show me somewhere you have visited... Now place yourselves around me to show me somewhere you think is special."

**2** The teacher stands in the middle of the room and says "I am in England (Ireland/Scotland/Wales). This is north, south, east and west. Place yourselves around me to show me a country you would like to visit... Show me a country you have heard about in the news... Show me a country you have a connection with (faith/family)... Show me a country you feel concerned for." The children, in turn say where they are and why.

**3** Some questions you might like to discuss:

> Did anything surprise you?

> Did you learn anything about your classmates that you didn't know before?

> What does this tell you about your class?

> What action would you like to take now?

*"You cannot teach a man anything. You can only help him discover it within himself."*

*Galileo Galilei*

*"Fulfilment of the 'I' can only occur through and in community. Self discovery and union with community grow in the same, not inverse, proportions. We can only arrive at our own 'unique self' by experiencing our existence shared with other persons. Therefore, the first purpose of community must surely be to help create a place in which the 'I' can be fulfilled."*

*Justice and Peace worker, Trafford*

# O ur bodies
**ACTIVITY 10**

 **V&V** This activity is about physical and emotional awareness, creativity and empathy.

"People have to realise that they can take their fate into their own hands. They have to recognise that they have the power to change society."

*Bertold Brecht*

## What are you doing now?

◊ You may be doing PE.

◊ In English you may be working on creative writing or reading stories or poetry.

◊ In history you may be looking at an event that changed society.

◊ You may be dealing with a conflict or personal difficulties within the class, school or staffroom.

## You might like to try  **C/A**

1  The class and teacher walk around randomly in a clear space. The teacher calls out an emotion, e.g. jealousy, and everyone moves around but now incorporating this emotion into their facial expression and movement. After 30 seconds or so a pupil calls out another emotion that they think of, perhaps excitement, and this is taken up in movement until another emotion is called out. Continue for perhaps a dozen emotions until everyone has the idea and is warming to it.

2  In groups, the children choose a favourite section of a lively story, or poem (from a number pre-selected by the teacher), or they construct a narrative from an event in history, the school, the neighbourhood or their own lives. The groups may do different pieces or all take the same story/event to interpret.

3  The groups create a performance in which the story/poem/ narrative is retold with each member of the group responsible for speaking one part while the rest of the group replay, through movement and facial expression, the emotions that underlie the action or poetic verse. They use their bodies to create an emotion-scape. Remind the children to explore movement as a group, not just as isolated individuals. Performances can be very powerful when groups use different but integrated movements, or strongly synchronised movement to express an emotion. At times it may be appropriate for the group to replay more than one emotion at once.

Comment: *It is important that the children do not confuse enacting action with enacting emotion; for example, a battle is embodied in acts of violence and avoiding that violence, but the emotions running through it might include anger, fear, horror, courage, aggression, cunning, boredom, doubt, grief, triumph, relief etc.*

# Creating a sense of COMMUNITY in the classroom and school

Community is about:

◊ each individual being valued; celebrating diversity; people being unique within the greater whole

◊ inclusiveness, valuing every part of the whole; opening a door to the wider world; recognising and valuing our interdependence; actively seeking to include others

◊ relationships based on mutual respect and open communication

◊ conflict being recognised and worked through creatively; hurts being healed

◊ sharing resources, responsibilities, endeavours, values, visions, feelings, histories and cultures

◊ living, growing and changing individually and collectively

◊ a safe place and a challenging place where people can be fulfilled.

Community exists where there is a deep sense of wellbeing, where each person and group feels valued and each is able to be most fully themselves whilst, paradoxically, being one with another. A community might be the family, friends, class, school, neighbourhood, a group of endeavour, a faith group, a country, the world...

There are functioning 'communities', such as overtly racist or sexist organisations, that are oppressive, exclusive and threatening, but these do not display the characteristics of community as defined by this project.

Attaining community, as defined above, is a tall order, but as one theologian writes, "our culture is competent to implement almost anything but our culture is able to imagine almost nothing." [7] Schools do indeed exist where there is this quality of community, and if they did not exist we would need to imagine them and create them.

There are four skills that are crucial to creating a sense of community. These are **affirmation, communication, cooperation** and **conflict resolution**. There are countless excellent activities that are designed to develop these skills (see bibliography). This book does not attempt to duplicate them. With the National Curriculum these skills have become ever more relevant as children are required to work in groups and as teachers need to set up situations which leave them free to evaluate the children's work in class. With the global challenges facing us affirmation, communication, cooperation and conflict resolution become vital if schools are to prepare people for the world in which we live.

This section focuses on activities for creating community where we are - within school. The activities on their own will not be effective. If the structures and ethos of the school generate barriers, these activities will be but a tinkering.

Sexism and racism bring division, limitation and conflict to a school and bar the possibility of real community. Again, there are countless excellent resources for working on these. Sustained strategies for breaking down barriers must underpin all work on community.

Community is obviously not limited to school; in its broadest sense community is our one world. Beginning where we are, knowing in an everyday way what community is about grounds the vision of one world, one community.

Intercommunal and intra-communal strife is ever-increasing. Our ability to create and be members of inclusive communities has become something that is crucial to the wellbeing of our schools, our society and our world.

---

"The problem is that the lack of community is so much the norm in our society, one without experience would be tempted to think: 'How could we possibly get there from here?' It is possible; we **can** get there from here. Remember that to the uninitiated eye it would seem impossible for a stone ever to become a gem."

*M Scott Peck*

# C**ircle time for children**

 This activity is about the here and now. It involves listening, reflecting on experience, taking responsibility and acting on it; recognising that suffering and joy are experiences common to all.

## *What are you doing now?*

◊ You may be concerned with registration time; the end of the day or week; activities for wet play; RE.

◊ With adults you may be looking for ways to end your governors' meetings or staff meetings.

You will need a magic microphone. A magic microphone is any object, perhaps a stone or a shell, which can be held by the speaker to indicate it is their turn, or opportunity, to speak. When they have finished speaking they place the magic microphone back into the centre of the circle, or pass it to whoever indicates they want it.

## *You might like to try*

**1** Everyone sits in a circle and reviews the day or the week. Each speaks in turn, with no interruption. The use of a magic microphone may help here. Each says, "one thing I have enjoyed this week is ..."; "I didn't like it when ...". This is a time for each person to be heard. There is no elaboration, discussion or comment at this stage. Anyone who wants to 'pass' in the circle should be free to do so.

**2** After each has spoken the teacher asks the children to sit quietly for a moment and to think about some of the different things that have brought pleasure or pain to them and to others during the week. It may be appropriate for the activity to finish there on reflection, or it could move on to action.

"I am dubious as to how far we can move toward global community - which is the only way to achieve international peace - until we learn the basic principles of community in our own individual lives and personal spheres of influence."

*M Scott Peck*

**3** Teacher and children together jot down the things they enjoyed and the things they did not like, and display them as a class poster.

**4** As a class the children choose one thing that they enjoyed. They then brainstorm ideas for increasing or ensuring that enjoyment. They choose one thing they did not like and brainstorm ideas for decreasing or minimising it.

Comment: *Circle time is a very powerful classroom activity which enables all those involved, adults and children, to explore feelings, emotions, relationships and self-awareness in a safe, non-judgemental environment with opportunities to share sadness and joy, silence and reflection, celebration and fun. All the members of the circle need to be assured that they are able to pass on any activity that they feel unready to participate in. All are equally valued and listened to, and all agree to a few simple ground rules to enable the group to function.*

*As the teacher and pupils become more secure with circle work they will begin to appreciate all that it has to offer in a democratic, listening and caring community. It is likely to become a central part of the life of the class, and hopefully the whole school community.*

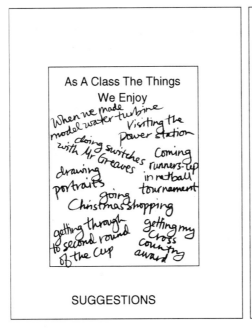
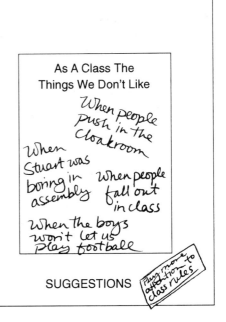

Thanks to a group of children in Wigan

# ACTIVITY 2
# uided fantasy
## - visiting an imaginary school

**V&V** This activity is about finding a shared vision; taking action based on one's vision; using creativity to bring about what you value.

## What are you doing now?

◊ With staff, governors, parents or children you may be trying to find common ground and a shared vision.

◊ Within the curriculum you may be doing design and technology work, identifying needs within the school.

◊ In art you may be examining your immediate locality.

◊ In RE you may be looking at how we live together.

## You might like to try $\boxed{A}$ [8]

1 Ask the group to sit in a circle. Explain that in a moment, if they wish to, you are going to take them on an imaginary journey to visit a school.

2 Ask them to sit comfortably, their feet on the ground, to close their eyes, to relax and to become quiet. Ask them to become aware of their breathing.

3 When everyone appears to be settled, read or invent a text similar to the following. Take your time, and give people time to imagine as you go along.

> I want you to imagine you are somewhere where you feel at peace. Choose the place you want to be. What can you see?... What can you feel?... As you look I want you to imagine that you can see in the distance a path that leads up a hillside towards some trees... Imagine you are walking along this path... There are fields on either side of you... The sun is shining... there is the sound of birds and insects...
>
> As you get nearer to the trees you see the path leading into the woodland... Please follow the path... The sun is falling through the leaves and branches making patterns of light and shadow on the ground in front of you... Walk along a little further until you reach another path that crosses yours... Here you see a signpost and on it is written 'School of the Future'. Please turn down that path... You may have to walk a long way... You are now approaching the school... The school that you are going to see is in the year 2010; it

"The school is a microcosm of the world. What we create in school can provide a glimpse of how our world may be."

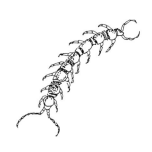

has been working for many years on values; it is an ideal and peaceful school. You are now going to visit this school, see the children, the women and men learning and teaching there.

You are approaching the school now... What can you see?... Go right into the school... What can you hear?... What can you smell?... What can you see?... Touch a few things... You can see the children and teachers now... What are they doing?... Can you see their faces?... Their hands?... Perhaps some of them are talking... What else can you see?...

Leave that group and wander through the school for a few moments and look at the children as you go... Who are the other people that you see?... Touch the books and things that children and adults will be using... Have a good look around... What is it like in this place?... What sort of feelings do you have?... What is the most important thing that you have seen?... Have a last look around now because soon you will be leaving...

In a moment I want you to open your eyes, and when you do you will be back here... When you are ready, please open your eyes.

Thanks to teachers and others in Derry, Northern Ireland, summer 1992

4 When they open their eyes ask them gently to feed back, without comment, all they saw, heard, touched and sensed. Write these up under an umbrella.

5 Ask people to identify:

  those elements they already have;

  those elements they can, with colleagues, create.

As they call these out, ring them so that it can be seen just how much is indeed possible.

**6** Ask people to reflect individually on, and jot down:

what element in the future school they most value;

what they want to create;

what they will create.

**7** People share these with a partner. Any main points that have emerged are shared with the whole group.

**8** Ask people to begin to start planning for action; to write down what they will do, with whom, by when, in order to create what they want in the school.

**9** Ask them to share the commitments in pairs and then to choose one element to share in the whole group.

**10** Ask them to find a partner who will support them in their commitment, i.e. will give encouragement and enquire on progress over a period of time.

Comment: *This activity has been frequently used with adults but can be adapted to explore specific curriculum concerns with children.*

*Often people are surprised to find that their ideal school of the future is simply made up of many very readily achievable elements - utopia is not something great and incredible but something quite wonderfully ordinary and well within the bounds of possibility. The activity is about visualising, analysing, choosing, deciding and making a commitment to action. The difficult part is the follow through on action. For school teachers whose lives may well be overcrowded and bursting at the seams, it obviously helps if we tackle tasks in twos and threes to support one another, listen and be accountable to one another. Obvious though it may be, it is often overlooked in schools and isolated individuals strive to achieve what two or three could do swiftly and enjoyably.*

## W A Y S    F O R W A R D

| I shall... | this week | this term | this year | within the next 3 years |
|---|---|---|---|---|
| on my own | | | | |
| with the children | | | | |
| with colleagues | | | | |
| with others, eg governors | | | | |

"I invite you to step out of your gloom, citizens of the old continent: you have conquered everything and all you have gained is individual isolation. Now it's your turn to discover and regain for yourselves a sense of community with all humankind."

*Tomas Borge*

# Today's world is...

**V&V** This activity is about the here and now; issues of justice, peace and the environment in the wider world; reflection; shared values and visions.

## What are you doing now?

◊ You may be meeting with parents, governors and teachers in order to clarify values and priorities in the school.

◊ You may be working with children on values in English, RE or environmental studies.

"What does it mean to grow rich? Is it to have red-blooded adventures and to make a fortune, which is what brought the whalers and other entrepreneurs north? Or is it, rather, to have a good family life and be imbued with a far-reaching and intimate knowledge of one's homeland, which is what the Tununirmiut told the whalers at Pond's Bay wealth was? Is it to retain a capacity for awe and astonishment in our lives, to continue to hunger after what is genuine and worthy? Is it to live at moral peace with the universe?"

*Barry Lopez*

## You might like to try $\boxed{\text{A}}$

This invites us to relate what we do in school to what concerns us in our world.

**1** Ask people to sit quietly for a moment and to reflect on our world today - what are the words and images that spring to mind?

**2** As a group, brainstorm single words that describe today's world. With one person acting as 'scribe' group members, including the one doing the writing, call out ideas. There should be no comment or discussion about individual contributions. Limit the activity to a few minutes, depending on when the momentum of ideas dies away.

Thanks to a group of parents, governors and teachers in Trafford LEA

**3** Ask people to look at the brainstorm and consider in the light of it:

> which three qualities do you want children to leave school with?

> which three qualities would best equip your children for the world today?

> Ask them to jot down each quality on a card.

**4** In pairs look at the qualities, compare and explain why they were chosen, reflect on them and together come up with the one which matters most. List, without comment, for the whole group.

<table>
<tr>
<td>

**QUALITIES / VALUES**

we want our children to have

Tolerance Happiness Christ
Love Respect Wisdom
Sensitivity Thoughtfulness
Education
Truth Selflessness
Spirit of Self value
God Stability
Honesty Being secure
Peace of mind Freedom to
Helping others grow

</td>
<td>

**GIFTS**

for a child to leave school with

Compassion Knowing who they are
Knowing they are a special and absolutely unique creation
Joy Forgiveness
Hope
Thankfulness Wonder
Amazing Awareness
curiosity Knowing their
Listening worth

</td>
</tr>
<tr>
<td>Thanks to a Trafford group</td>
<td>Thanks to a group in Derry, Northern Ireland</td>
</tr>
</table>

"The distribution of wealth is central to the social systems of all peoples, and many indigenous peoples honour their social and ritual obligations towards kin or community by displaying generosity. In some cultures a person's prestige and standing is determined by how much can be given away. Among Pacific coast Americans this is known as the 'potlatch'."

*Gaia Atlas of First Peoples*

**5** Some questions you might like to discuss:

> What strikes you about the qualities chosen?

> How do the lists relate to what goes on in school?

> If the school has a faith position, how do the qualities relate to faith?

> How do you encourage these qualities?

> What does the school (teachers/parents/governors/children/ancillaries) need to do now?

**6** Brainstorm what action is required.

Comment: *People are often surprised at how universally shared some human values are. Sometimes teachers imagine parents are only interested in the marks and exam results and sometimes parents imagine teachers don't share their priorities that their children grow in happiness and love. This activity can break down some of the misconceptions between parents and teachers and bring out the shared values and vision whilst, at the same time, exploring ways of working together towards them.*

When I first introduced the idea of Values and Visions to my class of 9-10 year olds I wanted to make sure that I didn't force my own values onto the children; I wanted them to recognise their values and visions, to put into words what is important to them as individuals rather than their parents', teachers' or peers' views. When we first discussed our "values and visions" we decided to brainstorm things that we felt were important - beliefs, dreams, ideals, wishes for the world etc... The result was a quite extensive compilation of DOs and DON'Ts. Most ideas were preceded by 'Don't', 'Save', 'Stop', 'More', 'No'. For example:

| | | |
|---|---|---|
| *Don't kill animals* | *Save paper* | *Stop bombing* |
| *No dictators* | *Don't waste* | *Respect belongings and other people's* |
| *Don't treat people as though they are a piece of dirt* | *No cruelty to animals* | *Help the world* |
| *More schools* | *Save the world* | *Help at home* |
| *Less illness* | *No weapons* | *Save paper* |
| *No smoking* | *Stop polluting* | *Don't waste* |
| *Stop hunting* | *No homeless* | *More jobs* |
| | *Save animals* | |
| | *No sexism* | |

We decided to concentrate on the positive phrases such as 'Help', 'Save' and 'Respect'.

Each day as the children left school I asked them the questions "Helped? Saved? Respected?" and each child had to say one thing they had done to help, save or respect during the day.

*Teacher, Trafford*

# W hich community?

**ACTIVITY 4**

 This activity begins to look at cultural diversity and unity and the whole notion of community and a sense of self.

## What are you doing now?

◊ You may be doing some practical maths with work on sets.

◊ You may be studying your locality in geography.

## You might like to try  C

This is an activity which highlights the fact that we are each part of many different overlapping communities; that community is complex and may be defined in terms of geography, faith, culture, endeavour, interest, lifestyle etc.

**1** Ask the children to move physically into sets. For example, all those who live in a village in one set, all those who live in a town in another set, and all those in between or not sure in a third set. Other sets might include:

those who speak/do not speak more than one language;

those who go/do not go to a place of worship regularly;

those who watch/do not watch 'Neighbours';

cyclists/non-cyclists;

those who play/ do not play sport, music;

those who are concerned/not too concerned about environmental issues;

girls/boys;

humans;

those who have/have not relatives overseas;

those who are/are not members of Wotsit parish etc

**2** List the different sets identified.

**3** Some questions you might like to discuss:

which sets do you regard as communities?

what do you think makes a set a community?

"People are lonely because they build walls instead of bridges."

*JF Newton*

**4** Ask the children in pairs to draw Venn diagrams to show which sets, or communities, they themselves are in.

**5** Some more questions you might like to discuss:

Are you surprised by the number and variety of communities?

Which do you really enjoy being a part of? Why?

Which do you not really enjoy being a part of? Why?

Who are the people in this community who are not in this class?

Which is/are the most important to you?

Are there any communities that do not get on well together?

Why not? What can we do to change this?

**6** Discussion could be followed with the children painting a composite class mural of the different groups/communities within the class or school.

# A day in school

ACTIVITY 5

This activity looks at diversity, at a Southern [10] perspective, at how different communities organise themselves and have similar and differing values; at differences in resources.

## What are you doing now?

◊ You may be looking at an economically developing country as part of your geography work.

◊ In RE you may be looking at Christianity in other parts of the world.

◊ You may be working on 'time' in maths.

"Sometimes we can't pay the bus fares but we walk to meetings and spend a while talking and being together and it gives us hope to live."

*Colombia: A Generous Land*

## You might like to try

You will need: two sets of photos, one of a British school and one of a school in, say, Tanzania.[9] The photos of the English school could consist of photos taken of a typical day in the life of your own school.

**1** Mix up all the photos together and mount them in random order on sugar paper; number each photo and display them around the class. Alternatively photocopy both sets of photos and give a set of each to each pair of children.

**2** Ask the children to work in pairs and to do the following activities:

sequence the photos to show the course of the day in each school;

find pairs of photos, one from the English school and one from the Tanzanian school, which show a similar activity going on;

find photos which show an activity unique to each school.

**3** Some questions you might like to discuss:

How would you describe life for the children shown in the English school?

What is life like for the children shown in the Tanzanian school?

Does anything surprise you about life in the Tanzanian school?

How is the environment regarded in each school?

What is of importance in each school?

Is there anything that we can learn from each other?

What might each school hope for in the future?

Why is it that many children in the South never get near a school?

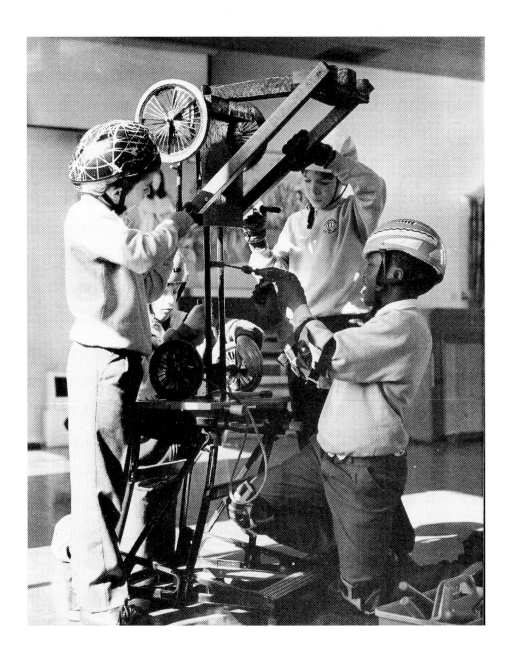

# ACTIVITY 6
# Living the day
## without the rest of the world

 This activity looks at deepening our sense of interdependence and dependence; acknowledging we are part of one creation.

## *What are you doing now?*

◊ You may be preparing an assembly.

◊ You may be working on geography.

## *You might like to try* C/A

For each person you will need paper and pen and a photocopy of a Peters Projection map (shown below).

1 Ask the group to think about their daily routines. Ask them to list what they do, what they use, what they eat, what they drink, what they wear from the moment they get up to the moment they go to bed.

2 Ask them to think about where all the different things come from and write the countries of origin next to the items.

"It costs £285 to keep a family going for a month, yet as a construction worker I earn £60 a month. It is the extended family economy which copes with things, but even then life is a misery. Such suffering over the past fifteen years, cutbacks in subsidies on basic food and medicines, the running down of the health and education services and all for what? So much sacrifice by the majority of people to meet the interest repayments on the debt (conditions imposed by the IMF), and nothing to show for it but mass exodus from the country and abject poverty for those who remain."

*Local community leader
Lima, Peru*

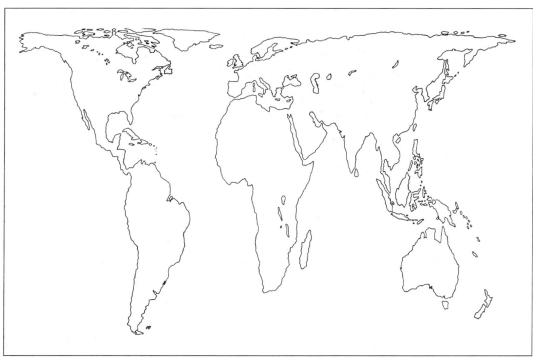

Traditional maps have tended to show countries incorrectly in proportion to one another, to the advantage of the European colonial powers, while the Southern [10] continents are shown far too small. This map, the work of Arno Peters, is superior in its portrayal of proportions and sizes.

**3** Ask them to try and live the next day without the rest of the world, in other words they must try only to use, eat, drink and wear things that were made, grown or produced in this country.

**4** As a group, discuss how the day went.

**5** Each person labels the map with the items they use in their daily routine and draws a line from each item to the country of origin. The maps from the whole group are displayed.

**6** Some questions you might like to discuss:

How easy was your day?

Did anything surprise you?

What did you miss most?

What did you miss least?

Has anything changed for you?

Is there anything you want to do now as a result of what you have learnt?

How do you think your daily routine compares with that of a person in another country?

# 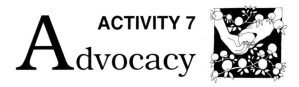ACTIVITY 7
# $A$dvocacy

 This activity is about listening, acknowledging feelings; forgiving and being forgiven; acceptance; here and now; fairness and justice; negotiation.

## What are you doing now?

◊ You may be trying to sort out the conflicts that have arisen during lunchtime.

◊ You may be doing RE work on the theme of forgiveness.

## You might like to try

"Oh God, help us not to despise or oppose what we do not understand."

1 When a conflict occurs in the classroom, each child involved chooses someone to be his/her spokesperson. One of the children in conflict presents his side of the story. The child who is spokesperson repeats what the first child has said, beginning "X says ...".

2 The other child in conflict presents his/her side of the story and the second spokesperson repeats what has been said, using the above format.

3 This process continues, allowing the children in conflict to respond to what they hear and express how they feel.

Comment: *The very fact that their point of view is listened to and taken seriously is often enough to diffuse tension and enable children to reach a mutually satisfactory solution to a conflict.*

"A whole bushel of wheat is made up of single grains."

A fable for community: The Prophecy

There was once a small monastery, a community rather down at heel that was thinking of disbanding. Then one night the abbot had a vision in prayer. The revelation was simple and short - "one of your number is the Messiah". He shared his vision with the rest of the community. And from that day onwards, things started to change because when each was with another member of the community they would think, "Perhaps this one is the One." So they began to treat one another with great love and care and respect. When they got up in the morning and looked in the mirror they thought, "Perhaps I am the One" and so they began to treat themselves with great love and care and respect. And so the community began to grow; people from far and wide came to join and soon the community that had been dying came to thrive, grow and prosper.

# Valuing the EARTH

> "Two men are at sea in a boat. One takes out a drill and begins to drill a hole in the bottom of the boat. The other protests, 'What are you doing? Stop!' The first replies 'Why should I stop? I'm only drilling under my own seat.'"
>
> *A Rabbinic story*

Earth is about:

◊ awe and wonder for the beauty of creation

◊ excitement for the miracle of life

◊ joy at being in the world

◊ respect for the living world and finite resources

◊ responsibility for the future

◊ the need for the just sharing of land

◊ awareness of being part of the web of life

◊ listening to nature.

There is an urgent need to awaken all people to their responsibility for the earth. This generation of adults is in a unique position. In our lifetime, a minority concern for the natural environment has transformed into the common recognition that the activities of an increasingly industrialised human race are destroying the ancient, elaborate and beautiful life system of our planet. How we now choose to treat the earth will determine whether the earth's fruitfulness is destroyed for ever. Children are well aware of this threat; they are the first generation to live with the question of whether the earth will be able to continue to support human life.

How the earth is treated is closely bound up with questions of who owns the land, who works the land, what sort of lifestyle do we want? Environmental questions are essentially about values, relationships, justice and peace.

There are many excellent resources designed to encourage a love for the earth and an awareness of how people's lives are being affected by the destruction of the environment (see bibliography). What *Values and Visions* sets out to do is to combine this awareness of what is with a vision of what we want for the future and a willingness to act on that in school.

This section will help to deliver the cross-curricular themes of Citizenship (Community Understanding in Wales), Environmental Awareness and Economic and Industrial Understanding.

# $\text{H}$eartbeat of a tree

 This activity is about wonder; creation and listening.

## What are you doing now?

◊  In science you may be looking at the process of life.

◊  In RE you may be developing an awareness of mystery.

◊  On a school trip you may be exploring the environment.

## You might like to try $\boxed{\text{C}}$ [11]

You will need a stethoscope.

1   In the classroom, listen to your own and others' heartbeats, and the heartbeat of the school pets.

2   Go into a nearby park or woodland area.

3   Choose a tree that is at least six inches in diameter and has thin bark (deciduous trees are generally better for listening than conifers).

4   Press the stethoscope firmly against the tree, keeping it motionless so as not to make interfering noises.  You may have to try several different places on the tree trunk before you find a good listening spot.

5   Some questions you might like to discuss:

> What did you hear?
>
> Did anything surprise you?
>
> How did you feel during that activity?
>
> What have you learnt from doing this?
>
> Will anything change because of this?
>
> What would you like to try next?

"Look thy last at all things lovely
Every hour."

*Walter de la Mare*

"Simple was my lodge of birch
Pure was the water that I drank

Swift was the canoe that carried me
Straight was the arrow that protected me

Wild was the meat that fed me
Sweet was the sugar maple

Strong were the herbs that sustained me
Great was my mother, the earth."

*Duke Redbird*

W̶e decided to do a project on trees. Each child in the group adopted a tree in the nearby park. They helped each other to measure their trees and had their photographs taken next to them. They made books shaped like trees, which they stitched together and decorated to look like their tree. In these they recorded the measurements, stuck leaves or seeds from the tree, drawings, diagrams, bark rubbings, descriptions of the wildlife that lived in it and poems they wrote about 'my tree'. Their faces were a picture the morning they found their tree covered in snow! Photographs had to be taken at once. They took a real delight in the life of their tree and a real pride in those books.

*Teacher, Wigan*

# $T$rust walk    **ACTIVITY 2**

 This activity is about trust, creation, sensory awareness, delight and wonder.

## What are you doing now?

◊ In science you may be developing the practical skills of observation of shape and texture using all senses.

◊ In RE you may be working on developing concepts of trust and responsibility.

◊ On a school trip you may want an enjoyable activity that helps the children explore the environment.

## You might like to try $\boxed{\text{C/A}}$

You will need blindfolds.

**1** Go out into a natural area. Get into pairs. In each pair, one is the leader and one is blindfolded.

**2** The leader guides her partner along any route, taking her carefully to visit any interesting objects and bringing her within range of interesting sounds and smells, shapes and textures, guiding her hand to explore them.

**3** After about 10 minutes swap roles.

**4** Some questions to discuss:

How did you feel during that activity?

Did you feel the same all the way through the walk?

What did you like/dislike?

What touch/sound/smell most interested you?

What was it like being blindfolded?

How would it have been different if you had been able to see?

Comment: *This can be a very refreshing activity, getting us back in touch with our senses. It also puts us in touch with our ability to trust.*

"There is not an animal that lives on the earth, nor a being that flies on its wings but forms part of communities like you."

*Qur'an 6.38*

"Allah did not want men to stop at looking after animals. Plants and trees needed care and respect, too. 'Even looking after plants and trees is an act of virtue,' said the Prophet. 'For a Muslim,' he said, 'it is an act of charity to plant a tree or till a land where birds or men or animals come and eat of its fruits'."

*Love All Creatures*

# ACTIVITY 3
# Sounds

 This activity is about creation, stilling and sensory awareness.

## *What are you doing now?*

◊ In science you may be developing observation skills and working on sound or materials.

◊ You may be developing an awareness of mystery in RE.

◊ On a school trip you may be exploring the environment.

## *You might like to try* C [11]

1 In a forest, meadow, marsh, park or piece of wasteland, people lie down on their backs with both fists held up in the air.

2 Every time someone hears a new bird song he lifts one finger. Who has the best hearing? For fun, see if you can count to ten without hearing a bird song. As a variation listen for general animal sounds or for any sounds at all - wind in the grass, falling leaves, rushing water.

3 Some questions to discuss:

How many birds did you hear?

Did the number surprise you?

How easy/difficult was it to recognise different birds?

What made it easy/difficult?

How do the sounds make you feel?

What have you learnt from doing this?

4 The class can also recreate the atmosphere or mood of the place where they lay with a soundscape. Objects from the place such as fallen leaves or branches, pine cones, rocks and gravel can all be used to make simple percussion instruments, as can objects from the school and home. Classroom instruments can also be used. The soundscape (don't forget the silences) is not a re-enactment, it is the recreation of a mood. The relationship between the qualities of materials and the quality of the sound they make can be explored, e.g. the soft timbre of wood compared to harder, louder sounds of metal.

"Kis-ne banaya <u>muchli</u>-ko, <u>muchli</u>-ko?

[Who made <u>the fish</u>?]

Kis-ne banaya <u>muchli</u>-ko, <u>muchli</u>-ko?

Hudda-ne banaya <u>muchli</u>-ko, <u>muchli</u>-ko.

[God made <u>the fish</u>]

Hudda-ne banaya <u>muchli</u>-ko, <u>muchli</u>-ko.

Repeat, substituting one of the following for the underlined word:

titlian (butterflies)

chirioon (birds)

p(h)ooloon (flowers)

hum sub (all of us)"

*Urdu children's song*

Kis ne banaya

# $\mathbf{M}$icro-hike

**ACTIVITY 4**

 This activity is about creation, global awareness and wonder.

## What are you doing now?

◊ In science you may be looking at the processes of life.

◊ In RE you may be developing an awareness of mystery.

◊ On a school trip you may be exploring the environment.

## You might like to try $\boxed{C}$ [11]

A micro-hike is a very short expedition around an open area of ground, guided by a string. The 'hikers' cover the trail on their bellies.

For each person you will need a length of string 1 to 2 metres in length and a magnifying glass.

**1** Ask people to span their strings over the most interesting ground they can find.

**2** Give each person a magnifying glass, to see things from an ant's perspective.

**3** Tell the group they must keep their eyes no higher than about 30 centimetres above the ground.

**4** Some questions to stimulate the imagination and creative expression:

What kind of world are you travelling through now?

Who are your nearest neighbours?

Are they friendly?

Do they work hard?

What is that spider going to do to you?

What would it be like to be that metallic green beetle?

Some ideas for creative expression based on Micro-hike:

Each person has a circle of paper to represent the magnifying glass. In it she paints the world of the ant she has seen.

Each person makes a collage of the world she has seen using fabric, paper, natural materials or a combination of these. The collages from the whole group are displayed together as one large collage of collages.

See also Activities 5 and 6.

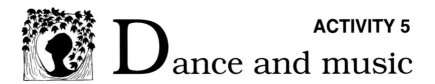

# ACTIVITY 5
# Dance and music

 **V&V** This activity is about listening, observation and empathy.

## *What are you doing now?*

◊ In music you may be exploring creating images in your mind and atmosphere around you.

## *You might like to try* [C]

1 Play a piece of music where the instruments suggest certain animals, their movements and behaviour. 'The Carnival of the Animals' by Saint-Saens is one suggestion.

2 Play the music again in sections (each animal separately) and ask the group to dance to it.

3 After each section: discuss the type of movements they made and the animal/s they think is/are represented. In what ways does the music sound like a particular animal? Which instruments are being used?

Some questions you might like to discuss:

How did they move? Quickly or slowly? Heavily or lightly?

Were their movements high up, low down or in the middle?

Did the creature move all of its body at the same time?

If several creatures move in a group, how do they move?

4 Ask the group to try out some movements from different creatures e.g. the ones they saw during the Micro-hike (page 45) emphasising that they are not miming the creatures but showing the quality of its movement, for example hurried and bustling for an ant.

5 Change from one creature to another. How does it feel to move in the different ways?

6 Work in groups of three. Ask each group to create a dance where they start with a clear shape - the resting shape of that creature. Then in their group, they should show movement, thinking about why the creatures are moving (fear, going somewhere, looking for food etc), and finally they should finish with a clear frozen shape.

7 Let the group experiment with different musical instruments and other sound-making objects to find which best express the movements of the creatures, and produce a dance piece.

# D ance and mime

 This activity is about creation, wonder, excitement at the miracle of life, and sensory awareness.

## What are you doing?

◊  In PE, dance or drama you might be representing the movements of animals and birds.

◊  You might be looking at dance of other cultures.

## You might like to try  <sup>12</sup>

Indian people have dances in which they show the natural world very beautifully.  You might like to try them.  This is what you do:

**1**  To represent birds, cross your right wrist over your left wrist. Face your palms upwards and link your thumbs together.  To show that the 'birds' are flapping their wings wave each hand gently and at the same time.

**2**  To show the graceful movements of a fish, cover your left hand with your right hand, both palms facing downwards.  To show the 'fish' moving, bend each thumb backwards and forwards.

**3**  To show flowers opening, put your fists together facing each other.  Then, very slowly, open your fists, keeping your thumbs and little fingers touching all the time.

**4**  To show the stars, lift both arms until they are at shoulder height.  Bend the wrists so the hands point upwards.  Now, to show the twinkling of stars, you slowly open and close your fingers. [8]

How could you use your arms and hands to show a spider, a beetle, an ant or any of the other creatures you saw on the Micro-hike (page 45)?

# ACTIVITY 7
# Webbing

 **V & V** This activity is about our interconnectedness, and respect for the interdependence of creation.

## What are you doing now?

◊ In science you may be looking at the processes of life.

◊ You may be exploring the interdependence of all life in RE.

## You might like to try ⬚ C ¹¹

You will need a ball of string.

1 Ask the children to sit in a circle. Stand in the circle, near the edge, with a ball of string.

2 Conduct a conversation along the lines of the one below:

"Who can name a plant that grows in this area?"

"Dandelion!" (Give the end of the string to the person who said it.)

"Is there an animal living around here that might eat the dandelion?" (You may need to hear a number of answers - select the most appropriate.)

"Rabbits!" (That person holds on to the string further up.)

"Now who likes rabbit for lunch?"

Continue connecting people with string as their relationships to the rest of the group emerge. Bring in new elements and considerations, such as other animals, soil, water and so on, until the entire circle of people is strung together in a symbol of the web of life.

3 To demonstrate how each individual is important to the whole community, take away by some plausible means one member of the web, e.g. a fire or a farmer kills a tree. When the tree falls it tugs on the strings it holds; anyone who feels a tug in his string is in some way affected by the death of the tree. Now everyone who felt a tug from the tree gives a tug. The process continues until every individual is shown to be affected by the destruction of the tree.

"...it is an important and special thing to be an Indian. Being an Indian means being able to understand and live with this world in a very special way. It means living with the land, with the animals, with the birds and fish as though they were your sisters and brothers. It means saying the land is an old friend and an old friend your father knew, your people have always known... To the Indian people our land is really our life."

*Richard Nerysoo, Inuit*

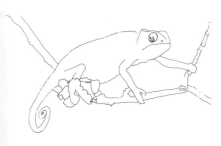

# ACTIVITY 8
# The banyan tree

 This activity is about interconnectedness, creation and empathy.

## What are you doing now?

◊ In science you may be working on the processes of life and interconnectedness.

◊ In RE you may be looking at environmental responsibility and care for creation.

◊ You may be practising listening skills.

## You might like to try C

**1** Read the story - The Banyan Tree:

There is a big tree in India. It is the banyan tree. It is in the forest. Many animals live in this tree. One day a man with a big axe comes along. He says, "What a big tree! I can cut the tree down and sell the wood in the market. Then I can get a lot of money and can buy: a house and land, some sheep and some goats, and get myself a wife."

The animals hear this. They come out of the tree. The tree is their shelter. Four little mice come first. They come to look at the man with the axe. They say, "Please don't cut the tree down. We live under the roots of the tree. It is our home and our shelter."

Then some beetles and moths come to look at the man with the axe. They say, "Please don't cut the tree down. We live in the bark of the tree. It is our home and our shelter." Then a swarm of bees comes to look at the man with the axe. They say, "Please don't cut the tree down. We live inside the trunk of the tree. It is our home and our shelter." Then some monkeys come to look at the man with the axe. They say, "Please don't cut the tree down. We live in the branches of the tree. It is our home and our shelter." Last of all, the birds come to look at the man with the axe. They say, "Please don't cut the tree down. We live among the leaves of the tree. It is our home and our shelter."

The man with the axe says to them, "I haven't got time to listen to you. I want to cut the tree down. Go away! I don't want to hurt you. Shoo!" The animals are very angry now. The birds peck at his hair. He shouts, "Ouch! Stop it! That hurts!" The monkeys throw fruit at him. He shouts "Ouch!

Stop it! That hurts!" The beetles, bees and moths sting his hands and fly into his face. The man feels scared of the animals now and runs away as fast as he can. The little mice can't do anything, but they say, "Thank you" to all the other animals.

They still all live in the forest, in the big banyan tree. It is still their home and their shelter.

**2** Act out the story in groups, freeze the action at various points and discuss the story with the group. Explore alternative directions for the story.

**3** Tell the story in comic strip form from the point of view of:

the man with the axe

the man's family who need the money he will earn

one or some of the animals

our point of view today.

**4** Discuss the idea of interconnectedness in relation to:

farming in our country or the developing world

the logging industry

stories known to the children from the press/media

exploration of a wood known or visited by the children.

Comment: *Concern for natural resources may bring people into conflict with powerful outside interests. The Chipko movement was established in 1973 to resist deforestation throughout Nepal and the Himalayan foothills. The Chipko movement uses a form of non-violent struggle: people link hands round the trees to prevent them from being felled. The movement looks back to an incident in 1730, when tribal women in Rajasthan embraced trees to prevent them from being felled for fuel for the Maharaja of Jodhpur's lime kilns; the women gave their lives, for they were cut down together with the trees. Their prayer was: "You guard us, you feed us, you give us the breath of life. Tree, give me your strength to protect you." (Moral Issues in the Hindu Tradition)*

"The Rock

The rock lays near
While light comes and goes

The rock only exists
Said to have no soul

The rock cannot be sad
It knows not the time

It has no life to hold,
it can't feel love as we admire it

It remains in stillness
Yet in its own way may watch!"

*Lloyd Carl Owle*

I had collected a load of sea-washed pebbles from a beach near my home in Wales and took them into a north Manchester classroom for the children to paint and make into paperweights. What I had not bargained for the was the interest there would be in the pebbles themselves. They were totally absorbed and there were shrieks of, "This one's got holes in!" and "Look! It goes black when you spit on it," "You can scratch your name on it with another pebble." Painting was abandoned till next time. It almost seemed a shame to paint them then...

*Teacher, Wales*

# Earth windows

 This activity is about sensory awareness and empathy with creation.

## What are you doing now?

◊ In RE you may be developing an awareness of mystery.

◊ On a school trip you may be exploring the environment.

## You might like to try  C [11]

You will need an area of forest, woodland or park with high bracken or long grass (and a spell of dry weather!).

1 Ask everyone to lie down, to look skywards and to begin thinking of themselves as part of the earth.

2 Cover each person's body with leaves, sticks and pine needles, right up to the sides of the head. Leave only the face exposed and use enough leaves and sticks to give a feeling of being down inside the earth.

(Work quickly and, in a large group, let people bury each other.)

3 Now ask people to close their eyes and place a few clean leaves over their faces, patchwork fashion.

4 Tell everyone you will give a signal when it is time to come out. Leave everyone for up to 20 minutes but stop before they get restless.

5 Some questions you might like to discuss:

How did you feel down there?

What could you see?

In what ways was it different seeing the world from under the ground?

How did it change how you saw and felt about things?

Did you hear, feel or see anything you did not expect?

Would you like to do that again? Why/why not?

What do you think life is like for the creatures of the forest (field etc.)?

Comment: *People will be much more agreeable to the idea of being covered with soil and leaves if they have been digging or crawling on the forest floor before the activity begins and if they are already familiar with various bugs and insects.*

"God is in the water,
God is in the dry land,
God is in the heart.

God is in the forest,
God is in the mountain,
God is in the cave.

God is in the earth,
God is in heaven...

Thou art in the tree,
Thou art in its leaves,

Thou art in the earth,
Thou art in the firmament."

*Govind Singh*

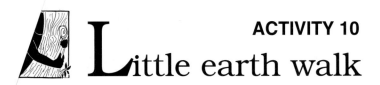

**ACTIVITY 10**

# Little earth walk

## What are you doing now?

◊ In science you may be looking at types of materials, shapes and textures.

◊ In RE you may be developing an appreciation of creation.

## You might like to try  [C] [13]

You will need a number of small egg boxes, a patch of ground, slips of paper in 15 sets of 5 (enough for a class of 30). Written on each slip is one adjective, e.g. rough/smooth/prickly/hard/soft.

**1** The children get into pairs. Each pair takes an egg box and goes outside.

**2** Each pair receives a slip of paper, on which is written a word. They then look for something on the ground which corresponds to the word. They show it to the teacher and then take a second slip of paper with a new word. Again they find an object that corresponds to the word.

**3** Having filled five spaces in the box they now find something else that they find really special to put in the sixth space.

**4** Bring the boxes back into class. Everyone places their special object in the centre. Take a moment to look at them all.

**5** Go round the class and encourage each person to say something about one thing that they found.

"Oh our Mother the earth,
Oh our Father the sky.
Your children are we, and with tired backs
We bring you the gifts you love.

Then weave for us a garment of brightness;
May the warp be the white light of morning,
May the weft be the red light of evening,
May the fringes be the falling rain,
May the border be the standing rainbow.

Thus weave for us a garment of brightness,
That we may walk fittingly where birds sing,
That we may walk fittingly where grass is green.

Oh our Mother earth,
Oh our Father sky."

*American Indian Prayers and Poetry*

# T he banks of the river

 This activity is about respect for creation, the need for justice, suffering related to abuse of creation, and Southern[10] voices.

## What are you doing now?

◊ In geography you may be working on pollution and protecting and managing the environment.

◊ In RE you may be looking at values, commitments and issues of justice.

◊ In economic and industrial awareness you may be looking at the concept of equality and freedom.

## You might like to try  [14]

1 Read this story from southern India:

> I live on the banks of the Tungabhadra River in south India. My Dad works in one of the two rayon factories higher up the valley. He hasn't always worked there - he used to be a day-labourer; that is, he used to hire himself out to various farmers, ploughing, weeding and harvesting their land. But it became very hard to find work. Some farms had been bought up by the factory owners and instead of food, the land was planted with eucalyptus trees. These trees are to use in the factories. They don't need much looking after so fewer workers were needed.

> Many farmers were no longer able to produce a harvest from the land so it was left idle and that put many people out of a job. In the end the only place to find work was in the factories.

> That's when my Dad went along. He earns enough to keep the family together, but our problems aren't over. My little brother is ill - no-one really knows what's wrong with him but he often has trouble in breathing. Many children in our village have the same problem. The school teacher says it's because of the factories. She took us outside the classroom and showed us how the clay roof tiles on the school are rotting. She also showed us the metal flag pole in the playground which is being eaten away. She told us that it is caused by the chemicals in the smoke from the factory. If

they have such an effect on clay and metal, what are they doing to us?

We used to go fishing after school, but now we keep finding dead fish floating down the river. We can see the thick black liquid that comes from the factory and kills the fish, but we have to water our gardens and drink water from somewhere.

Two years ago, the villagers got together. We sent letters to the Chief Minister; we had a procession to the office. There we burnt some rayon cloth to show our unhappiness with the factories. We stuck posters all over the district to register our protest.

But the factory owners threatened to sack anyone who took part in such protests. What is my Dad to do? If he stays at the factory, we have some money and can buy food. If he leaves the factory, where can we go?

**2** As a class, brainstorm all the possible different endings to this story. Choose the most desirable ending and think through what needs to happen for it to come about. A web chart would be a useful way to do this.

**3** Reflect on the story. In that situation how would you feel; what action might you want to take?

**4** Read the end of the story:

Now we are more hopeful. An organisation called India Development Service (IDS) was set up about ten years ago to work in our District of Karnataka State. With its help we have organised a village committee, one of a hundred in the region, each in a village affected by pollution. Because IDS is involved in the concerns of forestry and the environment, it has helped us to discover that the Indian Government has strict rules about pollution. It has helped us to find the best ways of letting people know when these laws are being broken by the factories. Now the factories have had to put in equipment to clean their air and water waste.

IDS is also helping us to find new ways to improve our environment. We are growing many new trees, not eucalyptus, and we are trying to raise new stocks of fish. The women are also learning how to spin and to start small dairy farms. This means they can earn some money and not be so dependent on their husband's earnings. Now we can afford to buy medicine for my brother.

**5** Compare the real ending to the story with the one that you as a class chose. In what ways are they similar? In what ways are they different?

**6** What do you think might be the next stage in the story? Write the sequel. Let children in the class choose to write both from the point of view of different people in the story and from the point of view of the river itself.

**7** Some questions you might want to discuss:

> Are there cases of pollution in your own locality?
>
> What organisations are there here that work on the environment?
>
> Looking back at the south Indian village, how did the community itself change in the course of dealing with the problem of pollution?

"We are the generation with the awareness of a great danger. We are the ones with the responsibility and the ability to take steps of concrete action before it is too late."

*His Holiness the Dalai Lama*

"May the great spirit
Watch over you
As long as the
Grass grows and
The water flows."

*American Indian Prayers
and Poetry*

A Rabbinic Tale

A wise rabbi was walking along a road when he saw a man planting a tree. The rabbi asked him, "How many years will it take for this tree to bear fruit?" The man answered that it would take seventy years. The rabbi asked, "Are you so fit and strong that you expect to live that long and eat its fruit?" The man answered, "I found a fruitful world because my ancestors planted for me. So I will do the same for my children."

EARTH
Page 56

# Developing openness to
# SUFFERING and JOY

> "Your joy is your sorrow unmasked. And the self same well from which your laughter rises was oftentimes filled with your tears. And how else can it be? The deeper that sorrow carves into your being, the more joy you can contain. Is not the cup that holds your wine the very cup that was burned in the potter's oven? And is not the lute that soothes your spirit the very wood that was hollowed with knives?
>
> *Kahlil Gibran, The Prophet*

Suffering is about:

◊ a spectrum of feelings from discomfort, irritation, frustration, anxiety, fear and loss, to desolation, misery, despair, pain and agony

◊ facing the uncomfortable and the unfaceable

◊ issues of injustice, violence and environmental destruction.

Joy is about:

◊ enthusiasm for life, enjoying life in its fullness

◊ a spectrum of feelings from savouring, delight, gladness, appreciation, contentment and wonder to happiness, thankfulness, awe, peace, wellbeing and celebration

◊ a sense that all is well and it involves looking for and valuing the positive

◊ finding hope in the world about us; a hope that is realistic about the degree of suffering that exists locally and globally.

Suffering and joy are inseparable and both are about:

◊ relationships

◊ the immediate, both local and global.

Suffering and joy, by their very nature, are often unpredictable, surprising and elusive.

In schools, as in the world, there is sometimes a numbness, a neutrality which is closed to both suffering and joy. The joy which, if expressed, might lead to a sense of wellbeing, gladness, thankfulness and fellowship gets shut out along with the suffering. The suffering which we bring with us into school and which is part of life gets ignored and may well insist on resurfacing in the form of bullying, resentments, anxiety, put-downs, irritability, boredom and aggression not only in the playground and classroom but also in the staff room.

The massive suffering within our own society and globally[15] remains half-seen through the media, half-invisible, confused, an area we do not really know what to do with. Many of the children we teach have direct experience of abuse, poverty and the consequences of unemployment; there are those who come to school hungry and there are a few who have a family member in prison. Illiterate in dealing with suffering within school we remain illiterate and unable to respond to the suffering in the wider world. This inability to respond to suffering is perhaps the most crucial challenge of this decade. Out of touch with suffering, we may well find that we are also out of touch with joy.

In this section we shall look at a few ideas that provide opportunities for people within school to begin:

◊ to recognise suffering in and around themselves, on their doorstep and beyond

◊ to believe there is a way through suffering

◊ to find creative and compassionate ways of facing suffering

◊ to share suffering in ways that create important links and bonds to raise the questions: Why is there suffering in the world? Who suffers? How do my actions contribute to or alleviate suffering?

◊ to recognise joy and delight around themselves, on their doorstep and beyond

◊ to be able to express gladness and appreciation in the ordinary and everyday

◊ to be open to joy and wellbeing

◊ to be able to share and enjoy fellowship

◊ to raise the questions: What brings joy and wellbeing? How do my actions contribute to bringing in joy and wellbeing?

Our focus may be ourselves, others, the family, the community, the wider world, the earth.

Much of what we do in this area of suffering and joy will not be done in specific activities but will be expressed through the hidden curriculum, and it will also colour how we teach the basic curriculum - which resources, stories and images we choose. History is an obvious example of a subject which lends itself to the exploration of suffering: the explorers[16], the industrial revolution, Victorian England can all shed light on suffering. Science with its emphasis on the natural world lends itself to the experience of awe, wonder, delight.

In this section we have tried to include activities that touch on both suffering and joy.

> "But all shall be well, and all shall be well, and all manner of things shall be well."
>
> *Julian of Norwich*

# T hinking back to a time

 This activity is about reflecting on experience, listening, acknowledging aspects of suffering and joy.

## What are you doing now?

◊ You might be doing language work with the children.

◊ You might be doing a staff inset on pastoral care.

◊ You may be tackling the issue of boys being aggressive and unable to express their feelings in non-aggressive ways.

## You might like to try **C / A**

1 Ask people to have a sheet of paper and pencil at hand, to sit comfortably and to relax and close their eyes.

2 Ask them a number of questions; after each question give them time to think and to jot down thoughts and feelings onto paper that they would later be happy to share with someone else.

> Think back to a time recently when you felt happy... what was going on... what were your feelings? (leave people time to jot things down). Think back to a time recently when you felt sad... what was happening?... what were your feelings?... Think back to a time you felt irritated... what was going on?... how did you feel?... Think back to a time you felt excited... what were your feelings?... Think back to a time you felt cross or angry... Think back to a time you felt anxious or frightened...

3 Ask people to go into pairs and share with a partner anything they feel happy to share. Are there any similarities? What are the differences?

4 Ask people to get into groups of four and for each person to share one thing that they have learnt from the activity.

Comment: *This activity overlaps with those from other sections - Self on page 3, Community on page 21, Listening on page 97. It seems essential to include within work on suffering and joy an activity which enables people to articulate their feelings. This activity is very specific: look back, see what was happening, begin to describe the feelings around the feeling. As with work on affirmation, children will need preparatory work on generating the vocabulary. A class 'feelings' word bank would help.*

"There used to be a lot of people here; kids splashing in the water, laughing, singing - but now they are all gone, nothing left now."

*Aboriginal Australian*

# ACTIVITY 2
# The leaf
## - seasons and cycles

 This activity is about contemplation, creation, beauty and change; it involves imagination, creativity and reflection.

## What are you doing now?

"Each experiences his humanness to the degree he can open to his joy and sorrow."

*Stephen Levine*

◊ You may be doing a topic on weather and seasons in science.

◊ You may be doing change and death in RE.

◊ You may be doing creative writing in English.

## You might like to try C [17]

You will need some leaves.

1 Place a pile of leaves, all of the same variety, in the centre of the room.

2 Invite everyone to take one, any one.

3 Ask them to look at their leaf carefully and to get to know it as distinct from any other leaf, for in a moment they will be asked to place their leaf back into the middle with everyone else's and then to pick it out again.

4 After a minute ask them to replace the leaves.

5 Ask them to close their eyes whilst you mix them up.

6 Ask them to open their eyes and retrieve their leaf.

7 Check that everyone has indeed found their own leaf.

8 Lead them through the following text:

> I want you to quietly examine your leaf... Get to know it even more... Look at its shape... its size... feel its weight...
> Notice the kind of edge the leaf has... It might be smooth, or jagged, or torn... Notice the veins... Examine both sides of the leaf... Gently feel each surface... You might like to feel it against your cheek... Notice how many colours there are, or different shades of one colour... Notice the patterns in your leaf... There may be patterns in the colours, or patterns in the veins... This leaf - given to you by a tree - is unique. There never has been one exactly like it and there never will be again. Place your leaf down in front of you. Now we're going to use our imagination. Sit in a comfortable and relaxed position... Gently close your eyes... and be aware of your slow steady breathing... Imagine you are that leaf...
> Feel what it's like to be that shape... that weight... those

"Enjoy the earth gently
Enjoy the earth gently
For if the earth is spoiled
It cannot be repaired
Enjoy the earth gently."

*Yoruba poem,*
*West Africa*

colours... You are a leaf on top of a tall tree... You're firmly
attached to a twig... and you're surrounded by thousands of
other leaves... all slightly different from yourself... Feel the
gentle wind on both sides of you... Enjoy the feeling... Is it a
warm wind... or a cool one? Now feel the refreshing rain...
washing you... making you shine... Listen to the splash of
the raindrops as they hit you... and listen to the droplets
splash off you onto other leaves... Feel the rain...
refreshing... gentle... cooling... cleansing. Go back to the
time in the spring when you were a bud... Feel what it was
like to be tightly closed up, safe and warm... Feel the
warmth of the spring sunshine making you want to open up
to this outer warmth... Feel the life force flowing into you
from your twig... Very, very slowly you open... The tiny
leaves within the bud start growing and opening... and you
are one of these leaves... Finally you're fully uncurled...
facing the sun... absorbing its rays... turning your pale
greenness into rich bright green... All through the summer
you live amongst all the other leaves... growing... feeling the
strength of the tree running through your veins... You feel
yourself moving in the breeze, light and graceful... still
firmly attached to your twig...

You have felt the sun... the wind... the rain... You are fully
grown... What's more you have a marvellous view from your
high position on the tree... What can you see?... Have a
good look around... Can you see the other trees?...Can you
see creatures in the tree?...What can you see in the
distance?... How wonderful to have such a view...!

Autumn approaches and you feel a difference... The strength of the sap surging through your veins ceases... You feel yourself drying up... Your bright greenness begins to fade... But you're aware of new colours appearing on your skin... Notice what colours they are... brown, or gold or red... or a mixture of colours... Suddenly, a strong gust of wind blows you completely free from the twig on which you've spent your whole life... the wind lifts you...You're completely free!... The wind carries you high above the trees... You twist... and turn... and float... and dance... Feel the movement... enjoy it...

Then the wind drops you and you float gently down... till you rest on the other fallen leaves lying on the ground... It's very peaceful here... What will happen to you now?... Do children come and have fun walking through the pile of leaves?... Or does some small creature carry you away to make itself a warm nest for the winter?... Or do you lie quite still, gradually rotting away until you become beautiful dark leaf mould which will feed the soil so that the trees may grow new leaves next spring?... Feel what happens to you...

Now we're going to leave our imaginary life as a leaf and return to the classroom... and now when you're ready open your eyes and stretch.

**9** After the visualisation, ask the children to brainstorm words that express their feelings at different stages of the growth of the leaf. The rules for brainstorming are on page 28.

**10** The children write poems of their lives as leaves.

**11** Some questions you might like to discuss:

Which part of the visualisation did you most enjoy and why?

Did all the leaves end up in the same way?

They all died yet their feelings were different. Why was this, do you think?

In what way is our life like or unlike that of the leaf?

Comment: *This activity may begin to help a child realise quite clearly the impermanence of life, the fact that all life is constantly changing and can be renewed. In relation to suffering this can help a child to realise that suffering will go away or change in some way. Further ideas for exploring the theme of life and death can be found in the section on Celebration and Grieving.*

# **M**editation on an image

 This activity is about contemplation and suffering.

## *What are you doing now?*

◊ You may be doing media work in English.

◊ In geography you may be working on an economically developing region.

◊ You might be doing RE work on responding to suffering; or work on the Beatitudes; or on Matthew 2:16.

## *You might like to try*

1 Choose an image that involves people in a natural disaster.[18]

2 Use a stilling activity (see the section on Stillness and Contemplation on page 129), with the children sitting in a circle.

3 Show the children the image and let them contemplate it for a minute. Invite them to be aware of their thoughts and feelings as they look at it.

4 Gather in and list some of the feelings and thoughts as a group.

5 Ask the children to work in twos and threes to study the picture and develop the story of it, including what is shown, what is not shown and what is out of the frame.

6 In small groups consider why this has occurred.

7 Discuss their thoughts and feelings. Ensure there is space for them to express their feelings and to have them heard.

8 Ask them to imagine the next bit of the 'story' and to make up a story as a group, a story in which some good emerges from the disaster.

Comment: *The aim of this activity is to begin to develop an empathetic understanding and compassion for destruction and death which is so much a part of the world. Children are bombarded by images from the media but are given little support in making sense of those images. The result can be a numbness and an inability to be open to facing the suffering in the world.*

"Deep peace of the running wave to you;

deep peace of the flowing air to you;

deep peace of the quiet earth to you;

deep peace of the shining stars to you;

deep peace of the Son of Peace to you."

*Celtic blessing*

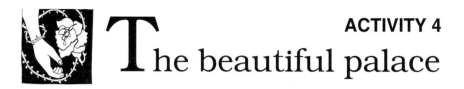

**ACTIVITY 4**

# The beautiful palace

**V & V** This activity is about justice and peace and creation; reflection and action.

## What are you doing now?

◊ You may be doing RE or an assembly on fairness.

◊ In geography you may be looking at how world resources are shared.

◊ You may be trying to help the children make sense of a piece of news.

◊ You may be working with teachers and governors on a mission statement for the school.

## You might like to try C/A [19]

**1** Read through the following fable:

There was once a king who built a large and beautiful palace and gave it to his four children to live in. The first brother to arrive took all the upstairs rooms for himself. The first sister to arrive took all the downstairs rooms for herself. They spent much of their time arguing and fighting, because each one wanted to be in charge of the whole palace.

When the second brother and sister arrived there were no rooms left for them. "As I am very kind" said the first brother to the younger one, "I will give you one of my very own rooms if you do all the work in the fields, growing all the food." [20] "I am very kind too," said the first sister to the younger one, "so I will give you one of my very own rooms if you do all the cooking and cleaning and washing."

Of course, the rooms offered were the smallest of the many rooms in the whole palace but the younger brother and sister had no choice if they wanted a roof over their heads. So they worked all day long, growing the food, cooking, cleaning and washing. They knew that this was not what their father had wanted for them when he built the large and beautiful palace, because he loved all four of his children equally. But the work was so hard that they were too tired to complain to their elder brother and sister.

When the elder brother saw the younger one become ill from overwork he said, "I will give him some medicine to make him better. I'm sure my father will be pleased with me for my kindness." When the elder sister saw the younger one was cold because her clothes were thin and worn out, she said, "I will give her the black coat that has got too tight for me. I'm sure my father will be pleased with me for my kindness."

Then, one day, when nobody was expecting him, the king arrived at the palace to visit his children.

**2** Go into small groups to make up the end of the story.

**3** Present it to the whole group either as a tableau or as a drama.

**4** Some questions you might like to discuss:

Have you ever been treated unfairly?

How did you feel?

How fair are older brothers and sisters?

How might things be fairer between brothers and sisters?

What might teachers and parents do to prevent unfairness?

Did the older brother and sister think they had behaved well?

If so, why did they think this?

Do people who do unfair things know that they are being unfair?

If they do not know, why do they not know?

How might they find out that it is unfair?

Do you know anyone who is treated unfairly?

Whose fault is it?

What about other people in this country and elsewhere in the world?

What can be done to put things right?

What is the large and beautiful palace?

If you were the younger brother or sister, what would you do to change things for the better?

What is the human family?

Who do you think does do most of the work in the world?

Who does the unseen work at school?

**5** As a group think of an area of unfairness in the school and decide on some specific action to alleviate it.

Comment: *The fable is of course a fable about the world and how the land, the resources and the work are shared out globally. Much of what is found at a global level is mirrored within school. And so when looking at issues of unfairness many teachers and children will ask to work on issues of gender. Why is it, for example, that the boys think without question that they can and should use up most of the playground? How is this in turn mirrored in the wider world?*

"Goodness is stronger than evil; love is stronger than hate; light is stronger than darkness; life is stronger than death."

*Part of a prayer of Desmond Tutu*

"You mean everyone isn't as happy as we are?"

*Tsering Dolma, a Ladakhi*

"We don't have any poverty here."

*Tsewang Paljor, a Ladakhi*

"If Ladakh is ever going to be developed we have to figure out how to make these people more greedy. You just can't motivate them otherwise."

*A Development Commissioner about Ladakhis*

# ACTIVITY 5
# Alemitu's story

**V & V** This activity is about suffering and joy, values and justice; it involves reflection and action; it has a global perspective.

## What are you doing now?

◊ You may be doing geography on an economically developing country.

◊ In maths you may be doing work on volume and distance.

◊ You might be doing English work on storytelling.

## You might like to try C [21]

**1** Read this story to the children.

> Alemitu lived in a village in southern Ethiopia. She was nine years old but had never been to school. She wished more than anything else that she could go to school for there was a school in her village. Her brother and some of her friends went there. But Alemitu could not go to school because her mother needed her for an important job - collecting water. Twice a day Alemitu went with her mother to the river to get water. It took them one-and-a-half hours to get there and one-and-a-half hours to get back, so that meant six hours walking a day just to get water. For people who lived further from the river it took even longer. Sometimes Alemitu was sick. People in her village often seemed to be sick. But she still had to go for water, because if she did not her mother would have to go even more.

> In the evening, Alemitu would watch her brother doing his school work. She watched him writing the Amharic letters in his book. Sometimes she would ask him what the words meant but her brother did not have the patience to explain. Alemitu wished more than ever that she could learn to read and write but she knew she never would. Her mother had never been to school when she was a girl and Alemitu knew it would be the same for her.

> One day, when she arrived back from the river with her water jar, she heard sounds of excitement in the village. A van had arrived from the town and people had gathered to watch as tools, ropes and other equipment were unloaded. "What's happening?" she wondered.

News went round quickly. Work was starting on a new well. Men from the village had talked about digging a new well for a long time, but they did not have the equipment or the special skills they needed. Now they had got help and were ready to begin.

Alemitu was so excited. She watched each day as the men from the village worked together digging deeper and deeper in search of water. She knew that, once the well was finished, she would not have to go to the river every day but just come to the well. People said that much of the sickness in the village would be prevented because the water in the new well would be clean and safe. Alemitu watched as the workers lined the inside of the well with special bricks. These would filter the water to make it pure. At last the day came when the hand-pump was fixed in place over the top and the well was finished. When the handle was turned, fresh clean water gushed from the spout. It was the most welcome sight Alemitu had ever seen.

She rushed back to the house to tell her mother. She knew there would be a celebration in the village. When she got home, there was a great surprise waiting for her.

"'Lord, when was it that we saw you hungry or thirsty or a stranger or naked or ill or in prison, and did nothing for you?' And He will answer, 'Truly I tell you: anything you failed to do for one of these, however insignificant, you failed to do for me.'"

*Matthew 25:44-46*

Her mother smiled and said she had something to give her. Alemitu waited eagerly while her mother took something from her basket and held it out to her.

Alemitu's eyes opened wide with delight. It was a school exercise book. She knew what this meant. At last her dream was coming true. Instead of walking to the river every day, from now on she would be going with her brother and her friends to SCHOOL.

2  Think back through the day; visualise all that you have done in the course of the day and note each time that you used water.

3  Now estimate the amount of water you individually and your class collectively have used today.

4  Measure precisely how much water you have used and compare with the estimate.

5  Go through the day carrying over a measured distance all the water you need in a bucket. Note the total distance covered.

6  Return to Alemitu's story. Individually or in pairs retell it in your own words as if you were Alemitu. Practise telling the story and then go and tell it to a younger class.

7  In small groups find out from the aid agencies such as Oxfam, Christian Aid, Cafod or Traidcraft about a number of water projects around the world. Decide which you think is the most important and why. Present the project to the class and decide if there is any action you want to take as a class.

8  List and celebrate some of the ways in which we use and enjoy water.

9  Discuss some of the issues raised by the story.

Comment: *This story combines both suffering and joy, the pain and frustration of not being able to do what you really want to do and the gladness when that frustration is removed. The story focuses on two basic human needs - water and education. Often the media presents a very dramatic side of suffering and ignores the more 'mundane' and widespread suffering caused by the simple lack of adequate water, adequate education and freedom from tiring and unrewarding work.*

"The person who does not wish to kill the smallest living thing knows what suffering is because such a person knows his own happiness and pain, knows others' happiness and pain. The one who knows others' feelings knows his own feelings. This is the way one must compare oneself with others."

*Acharanga Sutra 1.1.3.5*

# ACTIVITY 6
# Caged bird

 This activity is about justice and peace and the living world; it involves reflection and contemplation, beauty and creativity.

> "Spirituality is about well-being, being uplifted, relaxed, being in harmony with everyone and everything, being taken out of yourself, liberation, fulfilment."
>
> *Head teachers, Trafford*

## What are you doing now?

◊ You may be working on poetry.

◊ You may be doing an assembly on human rights and freedom around the time of Passover.

◊ In RE you may be working with the Bible on Exodus; a psalm such as Psalm 137; Matthew 25:35-46; Luke 1:67-79.

◊ In RE you may be looking at Judaism.

◊ In history you may be working on slavery.

◊ In English you may be looking at the media.

## You might like to try C/A

> "None of you has faith unless he loves for his brother what he loves for himself."
>
> *Hadith 2:6*

1 Overleaf is a poem by Maya Angelou. Read it to the class.

2 Let the poem do what it will; let the children explore the images and the feelings that the words and images evoke in them. When do the children feel free? Ask the children to use their own words and images to explore a song of freedom.

Comment: *Faith literature has much to say about freedom and liberation. 'Caged Bird' is very much within the context of the experience of black people. The poem can form a bridge over to the teaching about freedom within faith literature. It can also help us to begin exploring racism and its effects on people's lives.*

> "The spirit of the Lord is upon me because he has anointed me; he has sent me to announce good news to the poor, to proclaim release for prisoners and recovery of sight for the blind; to let the broken victims go free, to proclaim the year of the Lord's favour."
>
> *Luke 4:18-19*

# Caged bird

A free bird leaps
on the back of the wind
and floats downstream
till the current ends
and dips his wing
in the orange sun rays
and dares to climb the sky.

But a bird that stalks
down his narrow cage
can seldom see
through his bars of rage
his wings are clipped
and his feet are tied
so he opens his throat to sing.

The caged bird sings
with a fearful trill
of things unknown
but longed for still
and his tune is heard
on the distant hill
for the caged bird sings of freedom.

The free bird thinks
of another breeze
and the trade winds soft
through the sighing trees
and the fat worms waiting
on a dawn-bright lawn
and he names the sky his own.

But a caged bird stands on the grave of dreams
his shadow shouts on a nightmare scream
his wings are clipped and his feet are tied
so he opens his throat to sing.

The caged bird sings
with a fearful trill
of things unknown
but longed for still
and his tune is heard
on the distant hill
for the caged bird sings of freedom.

*Maya Angelou*

# ACTIVITY 7
# News from Pallem

 This activity is about suffering and joy and community; it involves story and a Southern perspective.

## *What are you doing now?*

◊  You may be doing an assembly.

◊  In geography you may be studying an economically developing area.

## *You might like to try*  C ²²

**1**  Read the story.  Different sections of the dialogue - or adapted versions of these - could be given to different class members to read out.  The details given in this story could be varied according to the teller's exact aims and objectives in using it. By inviting listeners to be the people in a situation apparently radically different from their own, the way is open to explore differences and similarities between the listeners and the villagers of Pallem.

> "I'd like to tell you a story about a tiny fishing village in India.  If you think of the land of India being shaped like an elephant's head, then Pallem is the bit below the elephant's right ear.  But instead of wasting time describing to you what the village is like, I would instead like to invite you to go there. (Show picture 1 overleaf.)  Imagine that you are a member of this family.  Just choose one of the people who you would find it most easy, or natural, to be.  The father is mending the nets, the son is tasting some rice, the daughter is sitting next to her mother who is sifting through some red chillies...

> "Imagine that you are living in a house where the roof is what the English would call thatched, where you are doing the washing up on the ground with metal containers. (Refer to picture 2 overleaf.) Just at the moment you are sitting inside one of the houses looking across the street.  You notice some branches blowing around; the tree is waving; some of the pans have turned over and are rolling down; a pole begins to crash down.  Yes, the wind is rising, the roof is shaking.  Before you know what has happened the roof of the house opposite is blown away.  Then suddenly your own roof lifts - there is total chaos!  A hurricane has struck - a

"Share in the suffering of others. Delight in the joy of others...

View the good fortune of others as your good fortune.

View the losses of others as your own loss."

*Li-Ying Chang*

Picture 1

Picture 2

devastating cyclone has ripped through the village!
Somebody shouts: "The boats are gone!" All the fishing boats
are washed away. There is complete confusion - animals,
children everywhere. The wind dies down and the chaos is all
around. You gather yourself together with one or two people
next to you. Somebody says: "We must send for help!"

"A young lad is sent as a runner to find a community worker
that some people have heard of. You begin to sit down and
discuss what you should do. There are so many things to fix
before life can come back to normal. All the boats are lost; all
the houses are destroyed and even the local church has been
blown to pieces."

2   So come back to being yourself and where you are. In groups or
three or four discuss what you would actually do. You can't do
everything at once. What will you put at the top of your list?
Rebuild the community building/church? Rebuild your own
house? Take a loan to buy new boats?

Listeners are invited to discuss amongst themselves. Give them
a time limit of, say, two minutes. Emphasise that there needs to
be group agreement for what is done. After the two minutes ask
who has decided to rebuild the community building/church. If
someone asks a question, wanting more information, say
something like: "In an emergency you don't normally know all
the facts. You have to work on what you've already gathered."
Concentrate not on what is right or wrong in the answers, but
why the group made the decision it did.

3   From the way that people are replying, the last piece of the story
can be told, weaving in insights already shared. The response of
the listeners half way through the story can be used by the
storyteller, and woven into the details of the second part, which
focuses on what actually happened. It certainly greatly
increases the quality and level of listening. Some thoughts may
be given to the authority of who is witness to these facts. It is
also possible to use the same method without images - relying
entirely on the group's imagination. Sometimes this can be more
powerful than using representational images such as
photographs. This is especially true if a group has developed a
habit of exploring and listening.

"When the community worker arrived (refer to picture 3
overleaf), she sat down with the various groups discussing
what they should do. Some people suggested that she might
be able to give them a loan so that they could rebuild the
houses. But after considerable discussion it was agreed that
a loan should be taken out to replace the boats, since this
was the source of food for the village. Secondly the
community worker suggested that the women form between
them a small co-operative to market the fish directly to the
nearby town, instead of the present arrangement which
depended on a middle person from outside the village."

Comment: *The person who tells the story needs to have further background details about the situation in order to reply to the questions; for example, the fact that the temperature is not very low, therefore people can survive for short periods without having their houses rebuilt, especially out of the rainy season. Once the boats had been purchased and the fishing continued, people found the time to rebuild their own houses. The money that was lent for the boats was put into a community fund. It was entirely up to the village to determine how this fund should be used.*

*The next priority was voted to be the building of a more permanent shelter, which would be used as a school in fair weather, but when the storms came everybody - each child, each animal, each living thing - could go into the shelter and weather the storm in safety. Having experienced how to work together and how to co-operate through this great disaster, the villagers went on to make further improvements to their water supply. They put their own labour and effort into laying a pipe several kilometres long which would supply clean water to the village to replace the rather badly damaged present system, which, in any case, was not very clean. You can see pictures of the boats and something of the way that they fished from the other pictures.*

# 100 blessings

**ACTIVITY 8**

and enjoying the moment

**V & V** This activity is about joy and creation; it involves reflection and contemplation.

## What are you doing now?

◊ Whether you are working with children or staff and parents, this activity will help to remind us about joy.

## You might like to try C/A

Throughout the day collect 100 blessings. Become aware of moments, events, encounters, things you see, hear, touch, smell, whatever brings delight, enjoyment or gladness. Note whatever is around you that is pleasing - the clouds, the wood of the table, the wind in the trees, the colour of someone's hair, the touch of water against your skin, a child's voice, a colleague's smile, something unexpected, something of beauty... Keep a mental note.

Comment: *Finding one hundred blessings in the day is a Jewish (Hasidic) practice. Complaining and moaning has become a habit in many places, including schools. This simple activity can change how we look at the day and can transform it. It can begin to bring into school a sense of gladness and thankfulness. If we wait until assembly to discover our capacity to praise, it may well have become rusty.*

"They are happy who are at peace with themselves.

To begin with oneself, but not to end with oneself;

to start with oneself, but not to aim at oneself;

to comprehend oneself, but not be preoccupied with oneself."

*Martin Buber*

SUFFERING AND JOY
Page 75

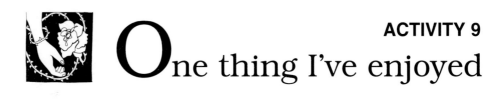

# One thing I've enjoyed

> "You will go out with joy and be led forth in peace. Before you mountains and hills will break into cries of joy, and all the trees in the countryside will clap their hands."
>
> *Isaiah 55:12*

 This activity is about joy; it involves reflection.

## What are you doing now?

◊ You may be starting off an after-school staff meeting.

◊ You may be ending the day with the children.

## You might like to try C/A

**1** Take a moment to reflect on the day and to find one thing that brought pleasure or enjoyment to you.

**2** Go round the group, ideally a circle; each person shares that one thing, putting it into a nutshell.

Comment: *At the end of the school day teachers may well feel tired. The things that have been difficult often come to the surface and crowd out any moments of enjoyment that there have been in the day. When first asked to do this exercise, teachers have often groaned, "But nothing went right today...". After a few moments of reflection they nearly always find something which has made the day worthwhile, but they have had to look carefully for it at times. Starting a staff meeting in this way means we start from a position of gladness. It makes it much easier to then go on and do the work of the meeting. People should, of course, pass if they want to.*

"If I had my life over, I'd try to make more mistakes next time. I would relax. I would limber up. I would be sillier than I have been on this trip. I know of very few things I would take seriously. I would be crazier. I would be less hygienic. I would take more chances. I would take more trips. I would climb more mountains, swim more rivers and watch more sunsets... I would eat more ice-cream and less beans. I would have more actual troubles and fewer imaginary ones...

If I had my life over, I would start bare-footed earlier in the spring and stay that way later in the fall. I would play hookey more. I wouldn't make such good grades except by accident. I would ride on more merry-go-rounds. I'd pick more daisies."

*Nadine Stair, aged 87*

# PART II

# Key Ways of
# REFLECTION

# Developing an awareness of
# ENCOUNTER

Encounter is about:

◊ relationships - how we relate to others and to the earth

◊ points of convergence: a meeting with a willingness to participate and with a sense of safety

◊ openness to change, exchange, balance, listening, a flow of energy, and the experience itself will be valued there and then

◊ shifts in perception, an acknowledgement of this, and a practical change.

Our lives are shaped by the continuous process of encounter with the rest of creation. When we are willing to meet with another person, other people or part of creation we enter into a relationship and through that we are changed. A teacher invites her class to look at a patch of grass. "What do you see?" "Nothing, Miss." The teacher lays a hoop upon the grass: the boys begin to look and to look some more; they look intently and are absorbed, caught up completely by what they see. "Miss, that's it, isn't it; everything is related..." Suddenly everything makes sense and that child's understanding of the world may never be quite the same again. The first look at the grass was just a look at the grass: the second time though bore the signs of encounter.

In the example above, the boys became willing to participate in the experience. They were open, they watched and listened, they valued what was happening, their perception shifted from 'we are all separate' to 'we are all interconnected'. That perception if kept alive will lead to practical change in the way that they relate to their environment and perhaps to others.

Encounter can happen almost anywhere within the curriculum or hidden curriculum. When planning or evaluating any activity, resource or input, we can ask ourselves where in all this is the encounter or the elements of encounter. It may be with the poetry in the English class or looking at the earth in a science class; it may arise during a conflict the lunchtime organisers are sorting out; it may be between the governors and the head, between the parents and the staff; it may be during an assembly; it may be with a character in history or within the Scriptures; it may be between the macho boys; or it may be in listening to people from the South. In any of these situations how do we create an opportunity for encounter, that is, a meeting in which there is a sound relationship based on openness, mutuality and exchange?

# S tructured interview

## What are you doing now?

◊   In RE you may be studying a faith such as Islam, Christianity, Judaism.

## You might like to try

You will need a visit from someone who is prepared to be interviewed about their faith, an artefact that relates to that faith and some cards.

**1**   Think of an object which is special to you, that has meaning for you.  For example, it might be a ring, a special book or a membership card.  Choose something and take time to think about why it is special to you and then write down the name of what you have chosen on a card.

**2**   Put the cards together into a bowl in the centre.  One person reads them out: these are some of the things valued in this group.

**3**   Find a partner and each in turn talk about your object and its meaning for you.

**4**   Now the chosen artefact, let's take as the example a Muslim prayer mat, is placed in the middle of the group and it is explained very simply that a mat similar to this one is used by millions of people throughout the world several times a day. Look at it carefully, think about it, what it might be, what it might mean for someone and then decide on a question that you want to ask.  If you could know just one thing about this object what would it be?  Jot down the question.

**5**   The guest to be interviewed now arrives, hopefully a source of answers to some of these questions but also much more than that.  They are not an answering machine; they may well have their own agenda, and things that they want to talk about.  But your questions are there for when the opportunity arises.  Listen and ask whatever questions arise.

**6**   After the interview here are some questions you might discuss:

   Was there anything that surprised you?

   What struck you most?

   What did you enjoy hearing about most?

   What do you feel you have learnt?

   In what ways have your perceptions changed?

"Everything is holy! everybody's holy! everywhere is holy! everyday is in eternity!

Everyone's an angel!"

*Allen Ginsberg*

Comment: *The faith or culture represented by the artefact chosen needs to be other than the predominance in the class so the structured interviews will be full of surprises. Usually they are a time when prejudices and preconceptions come tumbling down as we see the person behind the myth. When inviting a guest in, it is important to know who you are inviting and why. Talk over beforehand with the guest the objectives of the session.* [23]

*Obviously when you interview one person they are simply speaking as an individual. Just as no one Christian could possibly represent all Christians so no one Muslim can speak for Islam. Therefore, if possible invite more than one person in. They may well have different views on things and this will get over the fact that there is no one answer and things are not that simple. But they can begin to provide a glimpse of how as a human being they live their life and live their faith.*

*Often when talking with someone from a culture other than one's own, it is easy to get lost in generalities or little details. Starting out by thinking about the artefact such as the prayer mat immediately brings us down both to specifics and to an area of significance such as prayer.*

*Work on Islam is particularly important, given that countless Muslim children have suffered from racist abuse and attacks.*[24] *A look at Islam through something like a structured interview can not only begin to break down some of the prejudice and racism but also offer many important insights into issues such as responsibility for the environment, charity etc.*

*Structured interviews can be used in other contexts. For example, the class might want to interview the lunchtime organiser about her work; or interview an overseas student about their lives here and back home. In one school a Kenyan mature student came in and talked to the children and told stories. After it the teacher said, "the children will never look at an African in the same way again".*

# ACTIVITY 2
# The hoop

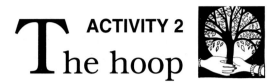

## What are you doing now?

◊ You may be doing biology or environmental science.

◊ You may be doing RE on care for the earth and our interdependence.

## You might like to try C

You will need a hoop for each person in the group, a dry day and a field or patch of grass.

**1** Go outside and find a place to sit on the ground away from other people.

**2** Put your hoop on the ground.

**3** Spend a few minutes in silence, looking carefully at what you see in the hoop.

**4** Rejoin the main group and share some of your thoughts.

**5** Some questions you might want to discuss:

How did you feel when you did that?

Did anything surprise you?

What did you hear?

What did you smell?

What did you see?

How do you feel now?

Has anything changed?

We were doing a topic about flowers, fruits and seeds and I'd planned a very simple lesson. Its aim was to encourage the children to look closely at something they see every day - grass! I led the children to a patch that was not really any bigger than the classroom and asked them what they could see. I got the expected replies such as "nothing", "just grass", etc. So I placed a small hoop on the grass, gathered them round and asked them again. This time with their attention more focused, they noticed far more - grass of different shades and shape, tiny flowers, clover, weeds, insects, mud, stones, etc. They seemed so pleased that there was so much there. Then they split into groups of two, three or four, as they chose and were given a hoop, some paper and coloured crayons. All they had to do was record what they could see in their hoop; discussion flowed easily. There were lots of gleeful shouts of, "Look, look a spider" or "Look, little flowers." One group of girls followed the route of a beetle for ages. Yet I was quite unprepared for the small group of boys who bounded over because they had seen a bumble bee on a flower. Rather than brushing it away, like children often do, they had sat so quietly and watched and actually saw it use its tongue to suck out the nectar and they were absolutely enthralled. Then, after a pause, Sean started a long and very complicated explanation that went something like this:

"That's it, isn't it? Everything is related. The bee gets the stuff and makes the honey and we eat it and at the same time it carries off the seeds and more flowers grow so there is more honey and everything is connected..."

It was like a light bulb going on; he clearly, for that moment at least, realised some of the interdependencies of our world and realised how vital that tiny bee was in a long chain of events. It started off from such a simple lesson.

*Teacher, Wigan*

# R ACTIVITY 3
## afa Rafa

## *What are you doing now?*

◊   You may be doing work on language.

## *You might like to try* C  25

You will need written instruction sheets as below and two groups of
up to 15 people.  Time: 90 minutes

INSTRUCTION SHEET for Alpha People

You are the Alpha people.  In your language, you add "-os" to
the nouns and verbs you say, e.g.  "I like-os bikes-os" or
"Give-os me some sweets-os please."

When you speak to someone you stand about two steps away
from them and you never look anyone in the eye when you
speak to them.  Looking people in the eye is considered very
impolite.  You usually bow your head a little.  You eat
vegetables, fruit and dairy foods but no meat.  You only drink
hot drinks like tea, coffee and hot milk.

INSTRUCTION SHEET for Beta People

You are the Beta people.  In your language, you say the
opposite of what you mean, e.g.  "I hate bikes," for "I love
bikes," or "Don't give me any sweets, thank you" for "Give me
some sweets, please."

When you speak to someone you stand very close to them and
you always look straight at someone when you speak to them.
It is very impolite not to do this. You eat lots of meat and
tinned foods.  You don't really like fresh food or dairy
products.  You only drink cold drinks and you especially enjoy
fizzy drinks.

**1**   Each group studies its instructions, practising the language and
asking for the things they like to eat and drink.  (15-20 minutes)

**2** Each group selects two ambassadors to go and find out as much as they can about the language, customs, food and drink of the other group. They should observe and make notes. They are going to teach their own group the things they have learned so that others can go and visit.

**3** Meanwhile, the rest of the group prepares a short sketch set in a shop. They are to come in, greet each other and buy the things they like to eat and drink. (10 minutes)

**4** The ambassadors visit other groups and the sketch is acted out for them. They observe and make notes. (10 minutes)

**5** The ambassadors return home and report. They teach their own group what they have learnt. (10 minutes)

**6** Two different people are selected from each group to go on holiday to the other group. They are to greet people, go shopping and buy food. The sketch is re-enacted with the visitors involved. (10 minutes)

**7** The visitors return home and report their experiences to their group. (10 minutes)

**8** If time allows, more visitors can be sent on holiday and the procedure repeated.

**9** Some questions you might like to discuss:

What did you like about the activity?

What did you dislike about the activity?

Did anything surprise you?

How did you feel during the activity?

What real-life situations are similar to this one?

Have you ever been in a situation like this?

How did you feel then?

Do you know anyone else who has been or is in this situation?

What have you learned from the activity?

# P ACTIVITY 4
## arents' evening
### simulation game

## What are you doing now?

◊ You may be having a staff meeting.

◊ You may be holding a school governors' meeting.

◊ You may be running an in-service training session.

## You might like to try A  26

Divide the group roughly into two. You will need for each "parent" a parent role sheet, a culture group role card (you may need to duplicate them), an adhesive label bearing their child's name and the number of the culture group. Each "teacher" will need a teacher role sheet only. Allow time for each group to study its role/culture.

---

**PARENT ROLE SHEET**

You represent a parent from another country or from another part of Britain. You are invited to a parent-teacher meeting at your child's school. Whether you are from another part of the world or from another part of Britain, you are completely unfamiliar with the cultural backgrounds of the teachers. In fact you assume they will be much like you. You feel that your cultural background is not the teacher's business and should avoid discussing it with her or him.

**PARENT ROLE PLAY**

You will receive the outline of a 'traditional' version of a member of a cultural group. Please study the outline and try to become that person for the duration of the simulation. Pay particular attention to the non-verbal action (or lack of it) that is typical of the role you are to play. You may wish to discuss how you will proceed with others playing the same role. Please stay in character until the simulation is over. Discourage attempts to guess what group you may belong to. In other words, stay on topic, which is your child and her/his progress at school.

You will wear a sticker that has on it a number (to differentiate among cultural groups) and a name, the name of your child. It is likely that the teachers will approach you and tell you which subject(s) they teach your child. Some of you may choose to make the first approach, rather than wait for the teacher(s).

---

"Work for peace within your household, then in your street, then in your town."

*Bershida Rabbi*

"The more I travelled the more I realised that fear makes strangers of people who should be friends."

*Shirley Maclaine*

**TEACHER ROLE SHEET**

You are a teacher assigned to a school with a large and varied ethnic population. The head teacher of the school has asked all teachers to attend an informal parent-teacher conference at the school to meet the parents. He has asked that through the evening each teacher engage each of the parents in personal conversation. You should discuss the parents' children with them and note whether they behave differently than you would under similar circumstances. You might ask parents about their ethnic background.

**TEACHER ROLE PLAY**

To make conversation starters easier, you could begin by introducing yourself as the teacher, naming your subject speciality. Each parent will be wearing a sticker with a number and the child's name.

Do not try to guess what cultural group each parent represents. Rather concentrate on the communication difficulties you are or are not having.

---

**CULTURE GROUP 1**

In your culture it is customary to bow slightly when you greet someone, rather than shaking hands. It is also your custom to stand about four feet away from a person during conversation. If female, you tend to defer to men, especially your husband, and those who you perceive as having status. You often express appreciation, even for small services and polite comments. You tend to nod your head or say "yes" frequently when you are listening. You smile not only when pleased but also when feeling self-conscious or embarrassed. You avoid direct eye contact.

---

**CULTURE GROUP 2**

In your culture people stand so close to one another that they can smell the other's breath, rarely more than a foot away. You engage in direct, long lasting eye contact that searches the other's eyes for meaning and emotion. You face people fully when speaking to them, eyeball to eyeball. Hand and head gestures are used frequently and physical contact/touching while speaking to someone of the same sex is considered quite normal. Shaking your head from side to side means "yes". You are not afraid to initiate conversation, even with relative strangers.

## CULTURE GROUP 3

Conversation is slow and measured and silences are considered positive communication. You feel that expressing one's emotions is rude and immature. You show few emotions through gestures or facial expression. Direct eye contact is considered rude or aggressive and viewed as a violation of private feelings. You like to stand close to equals, but not face to face. Instead you tend to turn your body away at an angle from the other or try to stand side by side. You cover your mouth when you laugh. It is of great concern to you that your child/ren not only do well in school but always obey and respect the teacher in all ways. Therefore, if the teacher were to report misbehaviour or lack of cooperation on the part of your child/ren, you would calmly assure the teacher that this will be looked into and resolved to everyone's satisfaction.

## CULTURE GROUP 4

In your culture it is not important to fill in time with conversation. Unless asked a direct question, you tend to remain silent. When in situations you are not familiar with, you tend to wait and watch to establish appropriate responses. If you are asked a question you carefully consider your answer before replying in a quiet voice. Also when shaking hands your hand may remain limp. Direct eye contact is avoided and may be seen as showing disrespect or aggression. In your culture children are given much responsibility for themselves at an early age and are expected to make their own decisions rather than always being told what to do.

## CULTURE GROUP 5

In your culture the acceptable social distance is about one and a half feet. You should always stand at least this close when conversing with another person. It is also customary to reinforce what you are saying with hand gestures. Conversation is rapid and spontaneous and interruptions are not regarded as highly rude. Emotions are displayed openly and touching is an important part of communicating feelings, especially with those of the same sex. You are not afraid at all to voice your opinion, especially where your child is concerned.

"Science has proved that if a body is to act upon another body, there must be continuity between the two. It is because of this law of continuity that we are all united to one another psychologically. If you smile at a baby, he smiles. If you put up an angry face, he weeps. If you sing, others also start singing."

*Swami Rama Tirtha*

1   Enact the role play using the role sheet and group instructions.

2   Some questions you might like to discuss:

How did you feel when you did that?

Did anything surprise you?

Which cultures did you feel most comfortable with? Why?

Which cultures did you feel least comfortable with? Why?

What have you learnt from this experience?

Will anything change as a result of this experience?

**ACTIVITY 5**

# Conflict tableaux

## *What are you doing now?*

◊ You may be responding to conflicts that have occurred recently.

◊ In RE you may be exploring attitudes and behaviour.

◊ In history you may be working on explorers.

## *You might like to try* C

**1** Ask the group to work in groups of three or four. Each small group thinks of a conflict that one of them has been involved in or witnessed recently.

**2** Each member of the group takes a role in the conflict and they work out a tableau or frozen picture to depict the moment of conflict.

**3** Each group presents its tableau to the whole group who have to guess what the conflict is. Questions are put to the characters to find out what they are feeling; what they were doing just before the conflict; what they are hoping for now. Suggestions are then made by the onlookers as to how best to resolve the conflict. When a suggestion is made, a member of the tableau is "unfrozen" to give her views on the solution.

**4** Each character in the tableau can think of something they might want to say at the time and on a given signal all shout it at once.

**5** This continues until a solution is found which is acceptable to all members of the tableau.

**6** Some questions you might like to discuss:

How could the conflict have been avoided in the first place?

What can we learn from these conflicts?

What good has come out of these conflicts?

How will we, as a group, respond to conflict in the future?

What action will we, as a group, take towards conflict in the future?

Comment: *The same technique can be used to depict conflicts in history, e.g. the arrival of Columbus or Captain Cook and their encounters with the indigenous population. Individual characters can be 'unfrozen' by a 'newspaper reporter' and her opinion elicited on the situation.*

# ACTIVITY 6
# Newcomers

## *What are you doing now?*

◊  In RE you may be looking at how we treat one another.

## *You might like to try* A

1  Ask people to recall situations in which they have been the newcomer such as joining a new club or moving to a new neighbourhood.

> How did it feel to be the newcomer?
>
> What did you say or do to get to know the people you were meeting for the first time?
>
> How can a newcomer let the other people know that she wants to join in?
>
> What can the people in a group do to make a newcomer feel welcome?

2  In small groups, short sketches are prepared.  In each, someone role plays appropriate behaviour as a newcomer, while the rest role play established members of the group.

3  The sketches are repeated several times with different people taking the role of the newcomer.

4  After discussion, the class draws up a welcome policy for newcomers and a commitment is made to welcome newcomers to the school.

5  Some questions you might discuss:

> How did you feel as the newcomer/established member?
>
> What would you like to happen in this situation?
>
> When might you be able to practise this way of behaving?
>
> What can we do to ensure that newcomers are made to feel welcome?

See also the section on Celebration and Grieving, page 151.

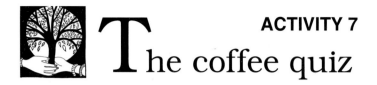

**ACTIVITY 7**

# The coffee quiz

## *What are you doing now?*

◊ You may be looking at world trade.

◊ You may be studying food.

◊ You may be learning about an economically developing country.

## *You might like to try* C [27]

1 Consider the following passage with your children:

> Every day we are linked to people in the Third World (or countries of the South, as many people prefer to call it). They touch our lives, and we touch theirs, when we use something they grew or made. You can see the end product - what you can't see so easily is what went into it, especially the price or wages paid to people in the South, and the conditions that they worked in.

2 Encourage the children to undertake some research by visiting the school or local library, or by writing to development agencies such as Oxfam and Christian Aid for information. Try to find out about some produce or raw materials that we all use which are produced by people in the South. How much do we pay for this produce? How much was the person paid who grew it or made it?

3 Make a display about the products based around a map of the world.

4 Try this quiz, then find out as much as you can about coffee production - even if you do not drink coffee you probably drink a fizzy drink containing caffeine, which comes from coffee.

**The Coffee Quiz questions**

a   Can you name three countries where coffee is grown?

b   Where did coffee come from originally?

     Ethiopia?  Brazil?  USA?  Spain?

c   How many people in the world depend on coffee for their livelihood?

     1 million?  5 million?  20 million?

d   Uganda depends on exports of coffee for what proportion of its income?

     20%?  95%?  70%?

e   What proportion of people in Uganda live off the land?

     86%?  100%?  20%?

f   Which country is the biggest supplier of coffee to the UK?

     USA?  Brazil?  Uganda?

g   How much of the world's coffee is consumed in the countries that produce it?

     22%?  80%?  100%?

**Answers**

a   Brazil and Colombia are the two biggest producers of coffee. Others are Mexico, Peru, Nicaragua, El Salvador, Guatemala, Costa Rica, Jamaica, Dominican Republic, Uganda, Rwanda, Angola, Kenya, Ethiopia, Cote d'Ivoire, Indonesia, India and Thailand.

b   Coffee is thought to have originated in the highlands of Ethiopia, over 1,000 years ago.

c   More than 20 million people depend on coffee for their livelihood.

d   Uganda depends on exports of coffee for 70% of its income.

e   86% of people in Uganda live off the land.

f   Uganda is the biggest supplier of coffee to the UK.

g   22% of the world's coffee is consumed in the countries that produce it.

# The coffee chain game

## *What are you doing now?*

◊   You may be looking at fair trade.

◊   You may be preparing a school assembly.

◊   In maths you may be working on simple statistics.

## *You might like to try*  [27]

You will need: a 100 gm jar of coffee, price marked as £1.60, a copy of the grid shown on the next page drawn on a flipchart or chalkboard with the proportion column hidden, a photocopy of the role-cards (shown on the next page) for each group.

**1**   Split the players into five groups and give each group its role card.

**2**   Give each group a short time to think about their role. What sort of problems might they face? What strengths do they have?

**3**   Hold up the jar of coffee, priced at £1.60. How much of the selling price does each group think it should get for the work they have done?

**4**   Each group takes a turn to tell the rest how much they should get. Encourage them to justify their claim. Record each amount in the "initial proportion" column of the grid.

**5**   Add up the amounts in that column - they may well come to more than £1.60! The groups now negotiate until the total reaches £1.60. Encourage discussion, discourage violence!

**6**   When agreement is (finally) reached, record the figures in the "negotiated proportion" column.

**7**   Finally, reveal the "actual proportion" column to show the figures different groups would receive.

**8**   Allow plenty of time for discussion after this role play and encourage the children to empathise with the real people involved in the coffee trade.

| | Initial proportion | Negotiated proportion | Actual proportion |
|---|---|---|---|
| Growers | | | 8p |
| Exporters | | | 8p |
| Shippers | | | £1.04 (shared) |
| Roasters | | | |
| Retailers | | | 40p |

## Role Cards

Give a photocopy of one card to each group.

### Coffee Growers

You live in a rural part of southern Uganda. You have about two acres of land to farm and your main source of income is from growing and selling coffee. You plant the coffee trees and weed the ground. The trees require lots of regular work and attention to keep them healthy so they bear fruit well. You harvest the coffee 'cherries' by hand when they are ripe. You dry them in the sun and sell them to a visiting buyer. The money you earn from the coffee is essential to pay for your children's school and the family's medical bills. Every 15 years you need to buy seedlings to replace old trees.

### Coffee exporters

You visit the growers to buy their coffee. The growers are scattered over a wide area, so you have to pay for transport and fuel to collect the coffee. Your factory processes the coffee 'cherries' to extract the 'green beans'. You sort the beans, pack them in bags, and transport them to the coast where you sell them to a shipping company. Uganda is landlocked and so you have to pay high rail freight charges. The market for coffee is unpredictable, so you sometimes have to pay to have it stored. You also need money to renew and repair expensive machinery in the factory and to pay skilled people to operate it

### The Shipping Companies

You buy the bags of 'green' coffee beans from the coffee exporter, load them on to your ship, and transport them to the UK, where you sell them to the coffee roaster. You have to pay highly skilled personnel to operate your ships. There are risks involved and you have to take out insurance for the ships and their cargoes, as well as pay for fuel. You also need to pay fees for using the ports, and taxes for importing the coffee.

### The Roasters

You buy the 'green' coffee beans from a shipping company and mix the different varieties of bean to get a 'blend'. You roast the beans and process them to make instant coffee then package it into jars and sell it to the retailers. It is a very competitive business and so you have to spend large amounts of money to advertise your brand and to provide attractive packaging. You constantly need to invest money to improve the taste of your blend and keep ahead of the competition.

### The Retailers

You buy the instant coffee from a wholesaler (the roaster), store it until you need it, label it with the price, put it on display, and sell it to the customer. You have to pay high rents to sell your goods at a busy location. You have to make your shop attractive, which means expensive decoration, and you need to train and pay a large sales force to provide a good service to the customer.

# Enabling
# LISTENING
## in the classroom and school

This is the Chinese character which means LISTEN
The section on the left denotes the *ear*
There are four sections on the right:

    the top one says *you*
    beneath that comes the *eyes*
    next is *undivided attention*
    at the bottom is *heart*

Listening is about:

◊ sympathy/empathy - understanding another's situation

◊ space

◊ tuning into a wavelength

◊ making an effort to understand

◊ love

◊ giving time

◊ contact

◊ quiet

◊ each person having their moment

◊ respect for the other person's feelings

◊ confidence in yourself

◊ eye contact.

*[Thanks to a group of Wigan teachers]*

In some cultures careful listening is a widely practised skill; there may be a strong oral tradition in which paper is less important than ears. Our western culture is not a particularly listening culture. We do not listen to anything very well in our modern, busy world. Words flow like water, much is jotted down on paper and passed around, but good quality listening is rare. Listening to another is really saying, without words, that they matter; it is being open to learning from them; it is being open to being changed by them.

When we listen, be it to ourselves, to each other, to others, to the South, to creation, to silence, we are affirming the worth of that to which we listen.

In school you may find that there are individuals and groups of people who do not listen to one another. Do you recognise any of these situations? Discussions in English are going awry because no one's point of view is being heard. There are girls in the class who cannot get a word in edgeways. Your maths and science group work is suffering for lack of listening. Playtimes are fraught because the lunchtime organisers are not listened to, nor are the children. After-school meetings are getting nowhere because the same people always dominate and conflicts simmer on as the divided parties do not listen.

This section offers a few activities that can help us to develop an awareness of listening, to practise the skills of listening and to use silence and stillness.

The activities in this section are illustrations only. You may well have ideas and activities that would be better, given your own situation. Use whatever works best, given the values and visions that you and those in your school have. Opportunities for developing listening are many: work on the news; listening to those groups within our immediate, local and global community who do not get listened to [28]; listening to the earth [29]; exploring sounds and silence; listening to self [30]; structured discussion [31]; listening to scripture [32].

Activities on their own will be ineffectual if the structures and the ethos work against listening. One can imagine the situation where the teacher shouts at the children "Sit down, be quiet and listen; we are going to do an exercise on listening, now be quiet." The important listening will go on outside any activities.

> "Focus on listening with one's whole body and being."
>
> *Teacher of special needs children, Manchester*

# Magic microphone

**ACTIVITY 1**

## What are you doing now?

◊   You might be running an English/RE/history class discussion.

◊   It could be circle time at the end of the day or week.

◊   You might be involved in a heated staff meeting.

## You might like to try  C / A

A magic microphone is any object, be it a special stick, stone, shell etc. which becomes endowed with significance.  Only when it is held can someone speak.

In a circle, people discuss whatever is the issue they need to discuss.

They only speak if they are holding the magic microphone.

When they have finished speaking they place the magic microphone back into the centre of the circle or pass it to whoever indicates they want it.

Comment:  *This very simple device rapidly raises awareness; the speaker becomes aware of the time and space that they are using. Instead of talk flowing like water rushing from a tap it becomes more measured.  It encourages those who ramble on or bluster to be more mindful.  It stops people from trying to interrupt each other and it precludes two conversations going on at once.  It makes for space between contributions and this sometimes makes it easier for a shy person to find their way into the discussion.  Overall, the magic microphone brings calm to the proceedings.*

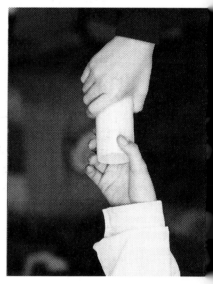

I use 'the magic microphone' every Friday morning after 'making friends' time as part of the recording of achievement process.

When our staff were discussing bullying we used creative listening so that people could listen to one another.  Otherwise we would all have been talking at once.

# Creative listening

## *What are you doing now?*

◊   You may be developing speaking and listening skills.

## *You might like to try* C/A

The group sits quietly in a circle, having agreed a time limit. Everyone is clear that they do not have to contribute verbally if they wish to pass.  When one person feels ready to speak they either simply start to speak or pick up an object like a magic microphone (see the previous activity).

When a person is speaking, the rest of the group listen.  They do not spend their time planning their responses to what is being said, and no one interrupts.

When that person has finished speaking (and has returned the microphone to the centre of the circle) there is a brief pause before the next person speaks.

When everyone who wants to speak has contributed, the group may feel free to spend some time in general discussion.

Comment:  *This very simple approach can have surprising results. The silence is the time in which reflection and creativity can occur. Instead of people batting ideas to and fro at a superficial level, it offers the space for reflection and for the spontaneous image to arise from within.*

*At first people may find this way of listening and speaking unfamiliar and uncomfortable, 'unnatural'.  However, this is not a good reason for not using it.  Immense discomfort and discord abounds in some schools, partly as a result of people not listening to one another, yet we continue not to listen.*

*With younger children someone may need to hold the magic microphone to make the quiet spaces.*

*Creative listening is no substitute for a vigorous, heated and swift exchange of ideas, but it does complement it and is of particular value after a conflict when no one has been listening to anyone else.*

*Both the magic microphone and creative listening are part of circle work.  This can be extended greatly.* [33]

"Most of us are so much thinking about our own ideas and points of view that we do not listen very attentively to others, unless we think they are experts.  For a spirit of trust and appreciation of one another to grow in a group it is essential that people listen to one another."

*Training for Transformation*

"True listening is love in action."

*M Scott Peck*

# Talk table

We were working on developing listening and tackling the problem of bullying. The children watched a video on bullying from the Islington Safer Cities Project.

One idea they saw was a 'talk table', a table where children who had fallen out could go and talk over what had happened. Shortly after having watched the video a table was placed outside one classroom by a teacher; on it was a notebook labelled talk table. Spontaneously children began to use the table; they would sit, talk, listen, make up by and large, or continue to feud. After using the table they entered their names and the date into the book and recorded why they had used the table and what had been the outcome. Some weeks later the children used their listening council to look at the pros and cons of the talk table. After careful consideration the children decided that they wanted to keep the table but that they themselves should think about the rules which would ensure it worked well.

*Teacher, Wigan*

# ACTIVITY 3
# Three tokens

## *What are you doing now?*

◊   You may be having a discussion.

## *You might like to try*  **C/A**

In a large group discussion each person is given three tokens (match sticks, beans etc.).  Each time they speak they 'spend' one token.  When they have used all their tokens they have none left to spend; they cannot speak and need simply to listen.

Comment:  *The tokens represent both the right to speak and also the responsibility to speak.  Some people will pause, think and weigh up the value of their speaking if they know that these opportunities to speak are limited to three.  Others who might have remained silent throughout have a tangible reminder in their hand that they, like everyone else, have things to contribute.*

"The eyes of those who see will no longer be closed, the ears of those who hear will be alert."

Isaiah 32:3

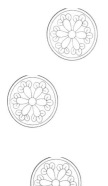

# ACTIVITY 4
# Active listening

## What are you doing now?

◊ You may be helping to resolve a conflict that has happened.

◊ You may be working on evaluation, profiling or records of achievement.

"Half an hour's listening is essential except when you are very busy. Then a full hour is needed."

*St Francis de Sales*

## You might like to try | C / A |

1 People choose a partner. In pairs they decide who is A and who is B.

2 Now B is to talk for two minutes about whatever is the issue in hand. For children it might be the fight that happened in the playground, the piece of news that was on television the night before or the piece of work they have just done. For teachers it might be around hopes and fears for a new curriculum initiative, or about a conflict within the school, or a difficulty that they are encountering with a child. B (Ben) talks and A (Ann) listens. But Ann listens in a particular way.

   Ann gives full attention to Ben, listening carefully and looking carefully.

   Ann sits next to Ben at a comfortable distance and ensures that there is eye contact (with staring) part of the time. Ann takes in everything Ben says and does not interrupt or add her ha'porth; she simply listens and nods or smiles as appropriate.

   When Ben has finished speaking Ann repeats back to Ben what she heard. Ben adds anything that he thinks Ann missed out or misheard.

3 Ann and Ben then swap roles; Ann speaks about something that concerns her and Ben listens and then feeds back to Ann what he heard.

"Give every man thy ear, but few thy voice."

*William Shakespeare*

LISTENING
Page 103

**4** Some questions you might like to discuss:

How were you listened to?

How did you listen?

What was it like being the listener?

What made it easy to listen? What made it hard to listen?

What was it like when you repeated back what you had heard?

What sort of listeners are we?

Are there any advantages to good listening?

"Listening is an art, a discipline."

*Training for Transformation*

Comment: *This is an effective structured way of helping people to listen to one another. The active listening involves us in using our eyes, ears, hearts and understanding, and both requires and develops empathy. When the listener repeats back what they have heard they will need to step into the speaker's shoes if they are to do it well and accurately. In a conflict it can help the person to really hear the other person's point of view.*

---

We will never give up on Listening Council

Children at a school in Wigan have written about their feelings concerning two activities used in their school, the Listening Council and Making Friends:

"Every week on Fridays every person in our class stands behind their chair and then Mr Coulson says go and make friends then a person comes to you and says sorry or thank you. The people who say sorry have either hurt you or done something like pinched your pencil... or if they say thank you it means that you're their friend or that you have been helpful."

"All of us thought it was a silly idea ... I (now) think making friends is great because you get all the horrible things that you have done out of your heads."

"Listening Council is all about getting your own say about what has happened, and is also to say what you agree with and what you don't agree with and also to give your opinion... I feel good to be actually talking to all the school... I like Listening Council and I would give it 10 out of 10."

# Listening Council

Staff and pupils alike have been amazed and delighted by the atmosphere at these weekly events. The Council meets for 15 minutes at 10.15 every Thursday morning and the children normally withdrawn for language help at the time are specially asked to join in 'our council' as they call it.

The meeting is in front of an assembly of all the upper juniors (two year 5 and two year 6 classes), a total of about 130. We meet in the hall in a very large semicircle with year 6 children on benches and chairs at the back and year 5 on mats on the floor at the front. This was to make it more comfortable than normal assembly, sitting on the floor.

Each class elects a representative boy and girl. Many issues of democratic representation, secret ballots etc. have arisen here. The eight reps (or listening councillors as some children have started to describe them) sit in a row at the front facing the assembly. We have dispensed with a chairperson as each speaker can choose who to pass the 'magic microphone' to.

The idea is that children listen actively to each other (not just sit quietly) and feel free to comment on the subject under discussion. In practice we start off with the reps at the front if they wish to speak but otherwise anyone in the whole Council can contribute. Some weeks the children are left to talk about whatever concerns them about school life. At the moment I am setting the agenda to provide feedback to our staff/pupil working group on bullying, attended by year 6 reps. One idea in use is the talk table where children can go and sign on in a book before trying to sort out problems by discussion. This seems popular and even quite successful.

Those teachers who have observed have all commented positively on the surprisingly high level of respect, attention and true listening that takes place. I try to encourage participants not even to put their hands up while someone is speaking, so as not to intimidate the speaker or give the impression (possibly true) that they are more concerned with their own next contribution than what is being said to them.

The Council will develop in its own new directions. Pupils may wish to discuss issues outside school life in the future. At the moment the evaluation shows they are overwhelmingly pleased with the Listening Council. For our part we have assured them that we will read the minutes they keep and listen to their ideas. They have always been clear however that the Council has no realistic power to make binding decisions.

*Teacher, Wigan*

**ACTIVITY 5**

# Valuing a vision

## What are you doing now?

◊ You may be working on raising awareness about listening.

◊ You may be supporting people in planning action.

◊ Children may be working on an ambitious long-term project or adults may be implementing a new initiative (in this case use only Stage 1).

## You might like to try C/A

People work in pairs; one is A (Ann), the other B (Ben). Ann will be talking about a project or something that she really wants to make happen some time in the near or distant future. Ben will be 'listening' in three different ways. The activity has five stages.

**1** Ann talks for two minutes abut what she is wanting and hoping to make happen. Ben actively listens with no interruption but encouraging Ann with whatever nods and smiles come naturally.

**2** Again, Ann talks, repeating what was said in stage 1. This time Ben interrupts every now and then to raise all the problems, all the reasons why Ann will not manage it.

**3** Again, Ann talks, repeating what was said previously. This time Ben ignores her completely.

Then swap roles; Ann becomes the listener, Ben the talker. Repeat each stage.

**4** Some questions you might like to discuss:

> How did it feel when you were listened to?
>
> What was it like when you were continually interrupted?
>
> How did it feel when you were ignored?
>
> What happened to your vision as you went along?

**5** Ann and Ben in turn state very briefly what it is that they intend to create and each is listened to encouragingly by the whole group.

Comment: *In stage 1, the listener may experience the strength and encouragement that comes when we are listened to by someone who is prepared to believe in what we are saying. Usually people find that as they are listened to their hopes begin to take form and substance and they feel more confident that they can indeed do what they are hoping and setting out to do.*

"God has given us two ears and one mouth, so that we can listen twice as much as we speak."

*Stages 2 and 3 are in themselves quite destructive; people may well have experienced their hopes and plans dwindle before the scepticism of others, but these are both ways of 'listening' or 'not listening' commonly employed in schools and elsewhere. How often have we leapt to raise objections and offered a 'helpful' critique? How often have we been too busy to listen at all, offering only an ignoring ear? The stage 2 or 3 listener may represent our own inner voices that belittle or ignore what matters to us. Much so-called listening is not listening at all - it's waiting to get one's own word in, or it's a cacophony of voices, inner and outer.*

*Going through all three stages can raise an awareness of how vital our role as listener is in assisting a project to get off the ground or in killing it stone dead. It gives an immediate experience of how empowering listening is and how disempowering non-listening is. Listening can be a veritable power point.*

# Listening to the South

## What are you doing now?

◊ You may be working on RE, English or geography.

◊ You may be presenting an assembly.

◊ You may be preparing a parent/school governors' meeting to offer a context and perspective for an issue.

## You might like to try C/A

1 Find stories reflecting a child's eye view of their life in a different part of the world. Christian Aid and Cafod (see the address list on page 227) offer many stories that focus on children and communities facing challenges in their lives. Look for the stories which raise issues of development, justice, power, suffering and joy.

*"If you have ears, then hear."*

*Matthew 13.9*

2 Read the story and ask the children to do any of the following:

To reflect on the story and relate it back to their own experiences and talk about that in pairs; to dramatise the story in small groups and present it to the class; in small groups to choose a moment in the story and present it as a tableau, i.e. as a frozen picture (see the conflict tableaux in the chapter on Encounter, page 90).

Each to choose to be a particular person in the story and then work in pairs, taking it in turns for one to listen and one to tell the story from their character's point of view.

In small groups to transpose the story to their own neighbourhood to retell the story, adapting it to make it speak from their own situation.

To use liturgy or prayer.

To brainstorm as many different possible endings to the story as possible and in pairs to choose their favourite ending and explain their choice to the class.

To use photos and posters to analyse life in the country where the story is set.

Comment: *This activity raises several questions; who do we listen to? Whose voices are heard in school? Whose stories are told?*

*If we are concerned to question the values of materialism, the voices of the South have something of particular value to offer us. If we are concerned to respond to global issues, both the poor here in our midst and in the South have much we would do well to listen to.*

*With adults a brief story, parable or fable can help the meeting to be open to question and to ponder. It might help to set the scene at the beginning of a meeting, or to raise a question mark at the close of a meeting. Anthony de Mello is a source of stories from many traditions (see bibliography). A story at the beginning or end of a meeting is an invitation to listen, to question, to move past the parochial, to relate the issue in hand to someone else's story.*

"To a preacher who kept saying 'We must put God in our lives,' the Master said, 'He is already there. Our business is to recognise this.'"

*Anthony de Mello.*

"One day as she was walking past the tree the monkey, who had long wanted to hurt her, threw a coconut at her head. She caught it, cracked it open, drank its milk, ate its flesh and used the empty husks as bowls from which to eat."

*A fable*

**ACTIVITY 7**

# Magic spot

## What are you doing?

◊ You might be working on science, RE, environmental or citizenship themes.

## You might like to try C [34]

1 Ask the children to choose a place where they want to be.

2 Ask them to relax and become aware of their breathing. Ask them to close their ears tightly with their fingers for a short while and become aware of how they feel. Ask them to open their ears again and become aware of sounds.

3 Now ask the children to become aware of their thoughts and feelings.

4 Reflect on the activity together, discussing what real listening felt like and what sounds they heard.

Magic spot

Thirty-six children from our school go for a week's Earthkeepers training every spring at one of the LEA's outdoor education centres, Low Bank Ground by Lake Coniston. Before they return they make pledges to reduce their own impact on the earth by consuming less energy and materials, to deepen their relationship with the earth, and to share what they have learned and experienced in the Lake District with their classmates back in Wigan.

The Magic Spot is one of the most popular of the 'experience' activities which provides a time of solitude in a special place which each individual chooses for the purpose. No other person should be visible and the exercise is repeated in different conditions, including one in the dark. The child sits quietly against a tree perhaps, and either looks and listens or just allows thoughts and feelings to come and go. Opportunities for writing poetry or diaries are provided, either during or after each visit.

*A Wigan teacher*

20·5·92     <u>Magic Spot</u>

My magic spot was in a field at Low Bank Ground. There is a wire fence by the side of me and a stile in front of me and ducks on it. I sat on a long flat stone with three small holes in the middle. I could see Lake Coniston from my magic spot. There were lots of mountains with their tops in the mist. I could hear the cars in the village across the lake. I could smell manure from my magic spot. I knew that it was helping the earth. The Gondola was sometimes on the lake. I thought about myself. Am I helping the earth enough? What can I do to help people? I thought about the wars in other countries and how stupid they are. I thought about people who give up their time to help children at activity centres. I thought about Jesus and how he didn't boast about the good things he did. I thought about how I can improve the thing I do.

When I am in my magic spot I felt sad and lonely. I felt like my only friends were the birds. I could hear animals and water running. A broken wall was by the river like a dam Insects flew about and pestered me when I was writing in my diary. The wind rustled my hair and kept turning my pages whe I was writing.

# Developing our understanding and use of STORY

Story is about:

◊ understanding your experiences through the telling of them

◊ listening to the voices of others and learning from their wisdom

◊ being open to the truth within a story so that the story becomes part of our own experience, tradition, history and culture

◊ community - the story-teller and the listeners or readers

◊ expressing the inexpressible

◊ imagination and creativity

◊ fun and enjoyment.

"Storying is a powerful way to offer insights into human experiences... Stories well told touch people: they resonate within people, because in the telling of something deeply human, that which is human is touched."

*Ted Aoki*

**S**tories, poems, fables and parables have the power to express the inexpressible. They invite us to enter other worlds. The important thing is to be open to the story, to the truth within it so that the story becomes part of our own experience. A story is a verbal symbol which acts on us and challenges or nurtures us.

In this section there are a number of stories and various approaches for working with them that you might like to try.

# H ACTIVITY 1
# eroes

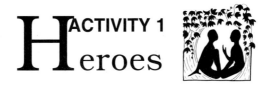

## *What are you doing now?*

◊ In language, you may be developing vocabulary for describing people.

◊ You may be telling a story.

◊ Perhaps you are thinking about what makes a good person in RE.

## *You might like to try* C

1 As you read a story, stop from time to time to elicit from the group what qualities they like or admire in the hero or different characters in the story:

What do you think about x?

Why do others in the story like her?

What helps her to do the things she does?

Who else do you know who is like that?

2 List the qualities on small posters which are displayed in the classroom.

3 The words elicited can be used in the affirmation activities described in the chapter on Self beginning on page 3.

"Everyone knows that stories are like spells."

*Nancy Martin*

Story-telling

"Our People have been using legends as a way of teaching ever since time began. Legends were told only during the wintertime, because that was the time for teaching, the time the children were inside the longest.

The story-teller was a man or woman who was well respected in the tribe. Sometimes they were parents or grandparents. The story-teller had to know the legends, history, be involved in tribal politics, religious ceremonies and be an excellent child psychologist. The story-teller had to learn to work well with groups and be able to sense the needs of the audience. They could read children by just observing them.

There were many lessons in the story-telling. Trickster stories, for example, have moral teachings. Raven stories are called 'Trickster Legends'. Story-telling brings generations together. The elders, parents and children all participated in the story-telling process. There were no generation gaps in our culture mostly because social functions were not age exclusive. Story-telling is an example.

Most legends stress that one should not be greedy, boastful, or make fun of others, especially elders, and that small beings could outsmart bigger and stronger beings. The legends also encourage older children to watch out for and help younger and weaker children. In this way legends taught the right way to do things.

Raven is the most infamous teacher of culture. Raven doesn't have an advanced degree from any college, has never sat on a committee, nor has Raven been asked to write articles, and yet Raven has been a primary teacher of our children throughout the ages.

Many tribes believe that when the world was young and being formed the animals were people. They could talk the same language, reason together, and cause things to change. It was the animal people who had to decide how long winter should be. The animal people went up into the sky to form stars, and some became mountains. This was a 'magic time' when the animal people had supernatural powers and could sway the world with change. Many times the animal people misused their power and really got into trouble."

*(From Positive Indian Parenting)*

# ACTIVITY 2

# Raven and the Sun

## What are you doing now?

◊ You might be doing work on story writing in language.

◊ You might be doing drama.

◊ You might be studying creation stories in RE.

## You might like to try C

1 Read and then act out the traditional story of 'Raven and the Sun'.

Characters: story-teller; grandfather (god-chief); Raven; Indians.

Props: a silver moon hanging on the wall, lots of tin-foil/glitter stars, a box for stars, a box for sunlight, a torch in a box that can be turned on for light, (fake!) furs and skins for Indians.

Story-teller: In the beginning, there was the great god-chief who had made the world. But alas, he did not give it light. Everything was in darkness. So Raven arranged to be reborn as the grandchild of the great god-chief.

Raven: Oh grandfather, you are so good to me! You spoil me and give me everything I ask for! Please may I have the moon?

Grandfather: Everything you ask for is yours. But you may not have the moon.

R: (pleading and begging) Please!

G: No! Leave me in peace!

R: (crying) Please!

G: Very well then. (Takes moon off the wall and hands it to Raven.)

R: Thank-you! (He rolls it around on the floor and tosses it in the air.)

ST: Suddenly Raven tosses it into the sky, right through the smoke hole in the roof!

G: (angry) Now look what you have done! Now my precious moon is gone!

R: I'm sorry grandfather.

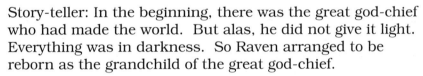

"This is our land. It goes back, a long way back, into the Dreamtime, into the land of our Dreaming..."

*Aboriginal schoolchild*

ST: But Raven wasn't sorry at all! He was happy that finally the poor Indians had some light in their dark, gloomy world. Soon he began begging for the stars.

R: Please grandfather.

G: No! Leave me in peace.

R: (crying) Oh please, please! I'll be very careful, I promise!

G: Very well then.

(He opens a carved box. Raven reaches in and scatters the stars in all directions.)

ST: Right through the smoke hole they went - all the stars lighting the darkness.

G: (angry) Now look what you have done! Now my stars are gone! You bring me great sorrow.

R: I'm sorry grandfather.

ST: But the cunning Raven wasn't sorry at all. Soon he began begging for the Sun.

R: Please grandfather - give me the box which holds the daylight.

G: Never, my child. This is my most precious possession.

R: Please!

G: No! Leave me in peace.

R: Please!

G: No, no, no!

ST: Of course the grandfather gave in. He could not refuse his beloved grandchild.

R: Thank you grandfather!

ST: And with those words the boy turned himself into Raven and flew towards the smoke hole.

G: Stop!

ST: The god-chief's power was so great Raven hung there and could not get away. His feathers were scorched and blackened! (Which is why all ravens are black today.) But he had powers of his own and wiggled through the hole to freedom. Off he ran carrying the precious box. At last he came to a camp.

R: Please let me have some food!

Indians: No. Go away.

R: (angry) If you don't give me food I will open this box and there will be daylight everywhere! You will be turned into animals like those whose skin you now wear.

I: (laughing) What? A boy like you with power like that? Go on! We don't believe you!

R: Very well then!

ST: And he lifted the cover of the daylight box! There was a flash like lightning! The people were afraid and ran away into the sea and forest. And sure enough, the ones who wore furs and skins turned into the animals whose furs and skins they wore. The people who wore no skins stayed as human beings. They adopted the animals as crests in memory of their relatives. And from that time on, there was daylight in the world.

*(Traditional story)*

2   Work in small groups. Each group thinks about something in nature and creates a story to explain it. The story is then prepared as a short play.

3   Each group acts out its play for the rest of the class.

4   Some questions you might like to discuss:

What do you particularly like about each play?

Is there anything you feel uncomfortable with? Why?

Tell us about any other stories you know of which explain why certain things happen.

"In all this teaching to the crowds Jesus spoke in parables; in fact he rarely spoke to them without a parable; thus making good the prophecy of Isaiah: 'I will open my mouth in parables; I will utter things kept secret since the world was made.'"

*Matthew 13:34*

"The disciples went up to him and asked, 'Why do you speak to them in parables?' He replied, 'It has been granted to you to know the secrets of the kingdom of Heaven; but to those others it has not been granted... That is why I speak to them in parables; for they look without seeing, and listen without hearing or understanding.'"

*Matthew 13:10-13*

# P ACTIVITY 3` arables

## What are you doing now?

◊ After a dispute, you may be helping the group understand a concept such as caring or neighbourliness.

◊ You may be looking at the Bible in RE.

## You might like to try C

"There are only two or three human stories, and they go on repeating themselves as fiercely as if they had never happened before."

*Willa Cather*

**1** Read the group a relevant parable. For sharing you might like to use that of the Good Samaritan in the New Testament of the Bible.

**2** Brainstorm together any images the group has of caring and neighbourliness, perhaps eliciting these with,

"What pictures do you see in your mind when I say 'caring'?"

"What people, animals, natural things do you imagine?"

"What pictures do you see in your mind when I say 'neighbour'?" etc.

List the responses.

**3** Now return to the story. Brainstorm the feelings of the people in the story.

What was it like for the priest and the Levi who walked past?

What were they feeling?

What did the Samaritan think when he saw the man in need?

What about the innkeeper?

What were his thoughts and feelings?

**4** In small groups people create a modern parable to explain the concept of caring for one's neighbour.

**5** The parables are told to the whole group and discussed.

Comment: *The parables are astonishing stories. Behind the nice, remote picture book version is a story which challenges and makes incredibly high demands.*

# Interview as story
**ACTIVITY 4**

## What are you doing now?

◊ In history you may be working on oral evidence about the way we used to live.

◊ In geography, you may be studying the locality.

◊ You might be working on narrative in language - describing experiences.

## You might like to try  C

You will need photographs or artefacts, provided by those taking part.

**1** Either singly or in pairs or small groups, people select someone they would like to talk to about their life. The person chosen might like to initiate the conversation by showing the 'interviewee' a photograph or artefact about which they would like more information.

**2** During the conversation, the role of the interviewer is to listen. Questions should be limited to requests for clarification and other comments to noises or gestures of interest and approval (see the section on Listening on page 97). It is important to conduct the conversation without taking notes and without the aid of a cassette or video recorder.

**3** Afterwards, away from the interviewee, the interviewer (each one individually if there were several) writes down or records on tape her interpretation of the interview, as a story.

**4** The interviewer returns to the interviewee and restarts the conversation by reading or playing the recording of her interpretation of the story. The interviewer listens again as the interviewee comments on the interpretation, but may prompt her on how she feels about hearing her story or if there is anything further she would like to tell.

**5** At the end of the second interview, the interviewee again writes down or records on to tape her interpretation of the interviews, as a story.

**6**  Some questions you might like to discuss.

>   What did you like or dislike about the interviews?

>   How easy/difficult was it to listen without comment?

>   How easy/difficult was it to remember what went on when you got back?

>   What was it like taking your story back to the person you interviewed?

>   How did the second interview differ from the first?

>   If several of you were involved in an interview, how similar were your stories?

>   If there were differences, how did they vary?

>   What have you learned about interviewing from this?

>   What have you learned about life stories?

Comment:  *This can be linked with the structured interview in the chapter on Encounter, on page 81.*

"If you want to come to know who you are... you might begin to reflect upon your own voice - the way you speak and write about your personal experience..."

*Ted Aoki*

# ACTIVITY 5
# Life stories

## What are you doing now?

◊ You might be writing autobiographies in language.

◊ You might be reflecting on joyful and painful experiences in life in RE.

## You might like to try **C** [35]

For each person you will need two small pieces of paper, a large sheet of paper and a pen, and crayons.

1 In groups of four or five brainstorm "Life is like..." (e.g. a gift, a journey, a jungle).

2 Individuals choose two of the ideas, one which they like and one which they do not like, and draw their images on separate sheets of paper.

3 In pairs, people discuss their choices and how they have shown them.

4 On the large sheet of paper each child draws a timeline of their life from the date of birth to today.

5 In the same pairs as before, the timelines are shared and feelings expressed.

6 The two pictures are then discussed in relation to the line.

7 Some questions you might like to discuss:

How easy/difficult did you find it to choose a picture to describe life?

How easy/difficult did you find it to draw your line?

How did you feel about discussing your life story?

How did the two pictures compare with the line?

Are there any changes you would like to make to the line now you have looked at the pictures again?

How does our picture of life/how do our feelings about life affect how we describe it?

"We are not mere smudges on the mirror. Our life-histories are not liabilities to be exorcised but are the very precondition for knowing."

*W Pinar*

"We Aborigines, we like to live the quiet way. We like to go hunting, to sleep in the bush and listen to the birds singing, the animals crying, stomping their feet on the salt plains... now we don't have those things. There's the noise of bulldozers and cars and aeroplanes."

*Joyce Hall*

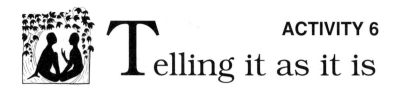

**ACTIVITY 6**

# Telling it as it is

## What are you doing now?

◊   In history or RE you may be looking at sources of evidence.

◊   In RE you are perhaps reflecting on how you see life.

◊   You may be investigating bias in books in language.

◊   You may be thinking as a staff about the staffroom.

"That really happened to me

I hope you like the story. Brian wrote that story whilst I was still hiding and it's true... I am Zeynep Hasbudak... Well, one day my dad went to the post office to get a letter. I don't know how they caught him but the police saw him and caught him. When my dad got caught he was in a prison. Then they sent him to Turkey. It was horrible. We were hiding but we were all crying and then I got ill and my mum got worried about it. So my mum said to the Home Office that she still thought they were being really really horrible but we agreed to go to Turkey. And we did."

*Zeynep Hazbudak*

## You might like to try   C/A

1   In a circle, the group is encouraged to close their eyes and relax and to reflect on their start to the day and their journey to school.

2   In groups of four, one person tells their story to each of the others in turn while the other two listen in. The first time the story is told, the narrator makes it sound dreadful, picking out all the things that went wrong. The second time the story is told, the narrator makes it sound as though everything was perfect, no problems. The third time the story is told, the narrator changes one element in the story.

3   The listeners reflect quietly on the three versions they have heard.

4   The group discusses the experience. Some questions you might like to discuss:

How did the three stories differ from each other?

How did each version affect you?

Which one is the real one?

How might this technique be used deliberately - who might do this for effect?

What does this activity tell us about life stories?

What can we learn from this?

How do you usually tell the story of your day?

# ACTIVITY 7

# What did they do?

## What are you doing now?

◊ In RE you might be reading a story from a religious text.

◊ In geography you could be learning about the effects of a natural disaster on a community.

◊ You might be responding to an item in the news.

## You might like to try C

1 Read the following story (or a similar one related to what is going on in class), stopping at dramatic points to elicit comments and discussion from the group.

### The Well at San Pedro [36]

"Little Carlos and twelve-year old Blanca live in a little village called San Pedro in Nicaragua. When the first well dried up, they had gone back to drinking river water. Then a brick factory had opened just round the bend in the river and several days each month the river was full of thick, dirty black oil. Everyone got sick. They longed to have a good well."

2 Stop here and engage the group in discussion. Some questions to discuss:

Have you ever had a stomach upset?

What did it feel like?

Have you ever been really thirsty?

Describe the feeling.

What did you do?

Have you had to do without something you really needed (e.g. food, water, electricity or gas cut off)?

What was it?

How long were you without it?

How did you feel?

What did you do about it?

3 Now read Ezekiel 37:1-14. This is a picture of a shattered and demoralised community recreated and restored by God. The message is spoken to a people who experienced great violence in the destruction of their home and the slaying of members of

their families. Such an experience is true of many in the world. The re-creation of a community is not just about working together but a task which requires common inspiration and collective energy.

**4**  Now encourage the group to reflect on the personal experiences in the light of the passage from Ezekiel.

**5**  Some questions to discuss:

>What sort of a picture are the words in the passage painting?

>How does it make you feel?

>How does this compare with how you felt when you were without something you really needed?

>What is the passage telling us about God?

>How did you feel when you got back what you needed?

>What should we do when we have not got something that we really need?

>What should the people in the story do?

**6**  Now continue the story.

>"The village met Jacinta when the first well dried up. They asked the INAA (the Nicaraguan Water Board) for help and Jacinta came along. At first the men said, "What does a woman know about digging wells?" But they soon discovered that Jacinta not only knew about wells but could also help the villagers look after their health. So the men and women began to talk to her. They decided to call in a water diviner to find water under the ground. He finally pointed to a gully about a hundred metres from the houses. So grandfather Tomas, Ramon and the other villagers began to dig again. It was very hard work digging in the sun-baked earth with only a spade as a tool.

>There had been more problems. First had come the hurricane in October 1988. There had been so much rain that the sides of the hole had collapsed and people were afraid to go down it. But grandfather and Ramon wouldn't give up and again asked INAA for advice. In the end they saved enough money to buy some cement. Carlos and Blanca had gone every day before school to help Ramon mix the cement and pass it down to grandfather who fixed rocks into the sides of the well to strengthen it.

>Then came the layer of solid rock. It was very thick and such hard work to dig through. But they'd done it at last, breaking it up with a hammer and chisel and bringing the pieces to the top one by one.

At last the water began to seep into the bottom of the well. They all thought the work was nearly finished, but Jacinta told them that having water wasn't enough - it should be clean water. They had to cover the well so that no dirt or insects could get in. They had to cement an area around the well, making a channel, so any spilt water could drain away. They even had to put a fence round it with only a small opening so that no animals could get in. The children's mother learnt how to test the water every day to make sure it was clean.

The pump came last. Ramon raised the pump handle and lowered it; then he raised it again. A stream of water gushed from the spout. The villagers cheered and clapped. Little Carlos, laughing with delight, ran to hold his face under the cool fresh water. Everyone began to sing and dance.

**7** What do you think happened next?

Comment: *The method used here is to oscillate between imagination and fact. First the audience is invited to enter into the story and to imagine their response in that situation and then they hear the facts - what actually happened. The use of scripture can help to place the story in a broader context of faith. This particular story could be useful in thinking about 'community' and how a community responds to a challenge. What are the challenges facing the community of which the school is a part?*

The story spirits [37]

Once long ago - was it in Vietnam or was it in Kampuchea or was it in Korea? - I'm not sure, but I do know that in a certain village there lived a husband and wife. They had one child, a boy, who was so fond of stories that he liked hearing them told even better than eating his dinner.

His father and mother made sure that, every evening, there should always be some neighbour who would come in and tell him a story. Most of these stories, which were usually about fox spirits or tigers (who were bad) and dragons or heavenly fairies (who were good), most of these tales were told at bedtime by a certain old man who often did work about the house and who knew a great many of the old stories.

Of course, this boy sometimes played with other children, and when they got to know about what happened every evening, they naturally wanted him to tell them the stories. But, beg as they would, this boy never took the trouble to tell them even a single one.

On the wall in one corner of the room in which this boy slept, there was a nail, and on the nail hung an old, forgotten, leather bag. Every time a new story was told in that room, the spirits from the story had to go into the bag, and because the boy would never pass on the stories to anybody, the unfortunate spirits could never get out.

As you can guess, the bag got terribly full, so that the story spirits had no room to breathe or move. There they had to stay, and the bad spirits - such as magic centipedes, foxes and, worst, the talking tigers - got more and more angry.

Well, the time came when the lad was old enough to be married. On the morning before the day fixed for the wedding, the faithful old story-telling man was stoking the stove near the bridegroom's old room when he heard a whispering. The old man listened.

"So he's going to be married?" said a discontented voice.

"Yes. A splendid wedding it's going to be."

"He's going to have all the fun, but we've been cramped up in the dark here - and some of us half dead - all these years."

"It isn't fair."

"We've put up with it too long. It's time we had our revenge. That's what I think." The old man looked into the room and realised the voices were coming from the old leather bag. He listened intently as he heard the voices plotting their revenge on the young man. One would become a drink and poison him, another would be poisoned strawberries, another would be a red-hot poker and burn him and a fourth would become a snake and bite him. The old man had to agree that the young man had done wrong to the stories, but how was he to protect him?

The next day he went with the wedding procession and snatched the cup just as the young man was about to drink. He refused to listen when he wanted to eat the strawberries he saw. He pulled away the sack the young man was about to step on to because he knew the red-hot poker was inside and he hacked to pieces the snake that was lurking under the bridal bed. The young man was furious and vowed severe punishments until at last he heard the old man's explanation and saw some proof.

Then the family begged the old man's pardon and immediately gave him a reward. As for the young bridegroom, he too thanked his old friend from the bottom of his heart.

"I am to blame!" he said. "But from now on I will tell stories to all who ask for them." Then he turned to his bride and comforted her, saying, "If we are blessed with children, I shall tell them a story every night! I shall tell them this story especially, so that no story spirits shall ever again suffer from being crowded up in an old leather bag."

# STILLNESS and CONTEMPLATION

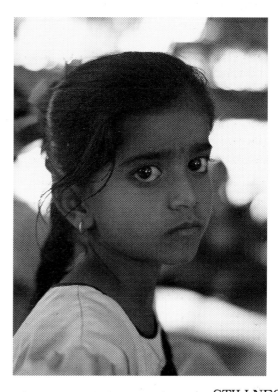

"A great Japanese master received a university professor who came to enquire about wisdom. The master served tea. He poured his visitor's cup full, and then kept on pouring. The professor watched the overflow until he could no longer restrain himself. 'It is overfull. No more will go in!' 'Like this cup,' the master said, 'you are full of your own opinions and speculations. How can I show you wisdom unless you first empty your cup'?"

*A fable*

Stillness is about:

◊ taking time and making space to make sense of experience.

Contemplation is about:

◊ taking time to be truly present in the here and now, to savour it, to enter into it, to allow awe into our lives.

Stillness and contemplation are about:

◊ making an empty space in our lives where we can respond to that inner sense of being part of something greater

◊ a way of life.

B abies and young children are quite often natural contemplatives. A baby will become completely absorbed in watching her own hands move, or the leaves shimmering in the sun and the wind, the cat licking its coat. The child will take time swooshing the leaves, savouring the lolly, splashing the water, gazing at this or that. As adults we are often busy and involved in doing, and will sweep up the baby or chivvy along the child... "Come on, don't dawdle," or "Stop day-dreaming," or "We haven't got all day".

Stillness, time for reflection, time to savour and contemplate whatever is happening is largely absent in our Western culture. We could learn much from the South.

In the busyness facts rush by and get lost. That 36,000 children under five die every day as a result of poverty becomes just one fact amongst a turmoil of other facts that fly past ungrasped in the flurry and confusion. The birth, the trees, the sky may all well go unseen as days fill with full agendas and important documents. Joy and suffering are crowded out and something unsatisfactory sets in. [38]

This section is about finding opportunities for reflection and for contemplation in school in order that:

◊   we regain a sense of refreshment and peace

◊   we integrate our experience into our understanding

◊   we get back in touch with who we are and what matters to us

◊   we are open to awe, wonder, compassion, surprise, insight

◊   we become aware of our inner creativity.

Stillness and contemplation are to be found throughout these guidelines. Ideally, they accompany almost every activity.

Now you may be concerned that with the many demands of the curriculum you would never find time for reflection and contemplation. Experience and research has shown that where they are used our learning and effectiveness increase remarkably. Strange but true - in less time we achieve far more! This is no doubt partly because through reflection and contemplation we become open to using all our creativity instead of just a little bit of ourselves.

The specific requirements for evaluation, assessment and appraisal within the Education Reform Acts are an open invitation for reflection and contemplation. The enormous stresses caused by the rapid changes being undertaken in schools call for a way of working which brings calm; the sheer quantity of curriculum demands requires the most effective and creative response. Contemplation is a much underused, powerful and creative human capacity. Let's use it.

> "Be still, and know that I am God."
>
> *Psalms 46:10*

STILLNESS and
CONTEMPLATION

# $\underset{\text{time and a place}}{A}$

## *What are you doing now?*

◊  You might be going through your everyday school routine.

◊  You might be in a staff, governors' or parents' meeting.

"In quietness and in confidence shall be your strength."

*Isaiah 30:15*

## *You might like to try*  C/A

1  Have a place in the school which is quiet and beautiful; a place where anyone can go, be they child, teacher, cook or head, to sit quietly, enjoy the flowers, read, pray or just find some peace and quiet.

2  Have a time in the day which is a quiet time; a time when all, be they teachers, lunch time organisers, children, find it is quiet, with people sitting reading or using their diaries, or walking or thinking through whatever they might need to think through.

3  Take moments before class starts or the staff meeting begins to stop and become still for one minute.  Do it regularly until it loses its strangeness.

Comment:  *Meetings usually get through their agendas quite swiftly when they set out from silence.*

STILLNESS and
CONTEMPLATION

Page 131

## ACTIVITY 2

# Body and breath

### *What are you doing now?*

◊ You might be in the middle of your everyday school routine.

◊ You may be involved in a conflict, or helping to resolve one.

◊ You may be winding down after an energetic PE class.

◊ You may be wanting to focus the group on a particular issue.

### *You might like to try* | C/A |

When doing this work, Anthony de Mello (see bibliography) suggests that we use "earnest playfulness".

**1** Ask the group to sit comfortably in a circle. Ask them to close their eyes, to relax and to become quiet. When everyone appears to be settled, read the following text out loud:

> "Now we are going to become aware of some sensations in our body... Become aware of the touch of your clothes on your shoulders... and of the feel of your clothes on your back... and now feel your back touching the chair you are sitting on... Become aware of the feel of your hands... let them rest on your lap... feel the air on your palms... be aware of your fingertips... Feel your shoulders... become aware of any tension in them... Now notice your thighs resting on the chair... be aware of the feel of the chair through your clothing... Now become aware of your legs... are they warm or cold?.. feel your feet within your shoes... and feel the floor beneath you... Go back to your head... become aware of the air on your face... feel the temperature... Go back down your shoulders... your arms... your hands... your fingertips... feel your spine... your stomach... your thighs on the chair... your legs ... notice any feeling in your feet... and as you continue to go around your body lightly become aware of each part and move on...

> Now become also aware of your breathing... notice the air as it comes into your nostrils... and become aware of it as you breathe out... Stay with this awareness for a few moments... simply noting each breath as it comes in and as it goes out... As you breathe in imagine you are breathing in light and energy... and as you breathe out imagine you are breathing out all anxiety and tension... stay with this awareness... and then when you are ready stretch, open your eyes gently and you are back here.

"Thirty spokes
share the wheel's hub;

It is the centre hole
that makes it useful.

Shape clay into a vessel;

It is the space within
that makes it useful.

Cut doors and windows
for a room;

It is the holes
which make it useful.

Therefore profit comes
from what is there;

Usefulness
from what is not there."

*Lao Tsu*

STILLNESS and
CONTEMPLATION

Page 132

**2** Give people time to talk about anything that came out of the exercise.

The following are quick variations on this activity which can be done at any time or in any place:

**3** Become aware of your breathing - stop whatever you are doing for a moment to take three deep breaths and to become aware of your breathing.

**4** Become aware of your body - notice where your body is tense. Squeeze up the muscles tight and then gently release them.

**5** Become aware of delight - take a moment just to look around you and to see the colours, shapes, textures and patterns that are right within view.

Comment:  *This exercise is a way of preparing for the guided fantasies in the visioning section.  Paradoxically, as we focus minutely on our bodies and our breath we become more able to venture out, to use our imaginations to go back or forward in time, to travel over the globe, to explore complex issues.  There are many specific exercises to aid contemplation.  These should be used with care and in context.  They may not be appropriate to every class.  As one head put it, "Respect the rights of the child; they have not chosen to be there; take care not to intrude or to use a powerful experience inappropriately."*

"His mother treasured up all these things in her heart."

*Luke 2:51*

"In, out,

Deep, slow,

Calm, ease,

Smile, release,

Present moment

Wonderful moment."

(with each word breathe in or out)

*Thich Nhat Hanh*

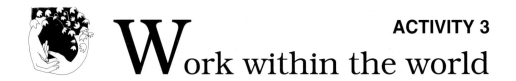

# Work within the world

## *What are you doing now?*

◊   You may be in the middle of your everyday school routine.

## *You might like to try*  C / A

1   Work within the world by taking time every now and then to stop and look at what is happening in the world, what is on the news, what people want to know about.

2   Stop and reflect on the issue, and place the school day within its context.

# J ACTIVITY 4
# ournals

## What are you doing now?

◊   You may be in your everyday school routine.

## You might like to try  C/A

1   Encourage the children to keep a journal to be written at the beginning or end of the day.  They might draw a diagonal line across the page.  Above the line they jot down things that went well and below it things they did not enjoy.  Feelings, hopes, fears are all part of the wholeness of the day.

2   Give the children time not only to write, but to reflect on what they have written.  How might tomorrow be?

Comment:  *The children should be under no pressure to share what they have written.*

STILLNESS and
CONTEMPLATION

**ACTIVITY 5**

# Staff review

## *What are you doing now?*

◊   You may be in a staff meeting.


## *You might like to try* $\boxed{\text{A}}$

Staff together take time to recall the past term, some of the achievements and struggles and failures; to recall the opportunities and frustrations, the people who have made a difference; the sort of ethos the school created; its purpose.

They then reflect on the present, on the current lifestyle of the school, the people within it, the opportunities there right now, the frustrations and tensions, the priorities and values.

They then take time to reflect on the future, to remember where they find hope and courage, to decide what their vision is, what their values are and how they will be part of the coming term.

# Developing
# SENSORY AWARENESS

Sensory awareness is about:

◊ acknowledging that we are human beings: creatures with arms and legs, with eyes, ears, noses, tongues and fingers

◊ becoming aware that all life comes to us through our senses

◊ using all our senses

◊ being open to experiences that come to us in a variety of different physical ways

◊ understanding more about our bodies

◊ being alive to the present.

This section outlines some activities for awakening a heightened sensory awareness, a greater appreciation of the world about us, but there are many other sources of activities. Earth education and the expressive arts in particular have many ideas to offer. See also the view of a teacher of children with special needs on page 163.

Coming to our senses, being more in touch with what is around us, relates closely to the sections on Earth (beginning on page 39), Listening (page 97), Stillness and Contemplation (page 129) and Celebration (page 151). This work can involve delight, wonder and awe, trust, appreciation and a growing awareness of ourselves as creatures who are dependent on an incredible creation.

"People tend to live in their heads - they are mostly conscious of their thinking and fantasising and not conscious enough of the activity of their senses. As a result they rarely live in the present. They are almost always in the past or in the future. In the past, regretting mistakes, bemoaning sins, gloating over achievements, resenting injuries caused them by other people, or in the future, dreading possible calamities, anticipating joys, dreaming of future successes.

Recalling the past in order to profit from it, or in order to draw strength from it by reliving its joyful moments; and anticipating the future in order to plan realistically - these are valuable functions, provided they do not take us out of the present for too long. The ability to make contact with the present and to stay there, is something you will have to develop if you wish to succeed in prayer. And the best way to make contact with the present is to get out of your head and come to your senses."

*Anthony de Mello*

# M̊irrors ACTIVITY 1

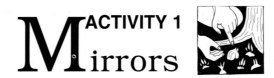

## What are you doing now?

◊   In mathematics you may be doing symmetry.

◊   You may be developing awareness of working with another person in dance or PE.

## You might like to try  C

People work in pairs and stand opposite each other, about a metre apart, hands by their sides.

**1**   One person is to lead and the other follow.  There must be no verbal communication.

**2**   Slowly the leader starts to move a hand and the other person mirrors the movement.

**3**   As confidence increases, the leader may move various parts of the body at the same time.

**4**   After a time the partners swap roles.

Comment:  *A further development can be for neither partner to be designated as leader beforehand, but one takes the lead and then the other as they feel the moment is right.  In this case the two partners are 'listening' to each other's body movements and learning intuitively when the moment for change has come.*

# T rust dance

**ACTIVITY 2**

## *What are you doing now?*

◊ In RE you might be celebrating your senses and thinking about what it is like to be without a sense, perhaps in relation to a story, such as Bartimaeus, Mark 10:46-52.

◊ In PE you might want to develop trust in preparation for co-operative movements in dance or gymnastics or to improve group work and cooperation in class in general.

(You may also like to use Trust Walk in the Earth section, page 43.)

## *You might like to try*  C

1 The group works in pairs. One, blindfolded, is 'unsighted'.

2 The leader makes a shape with his body in which he feels stable, secure and able to support the weight of another person.

3 The 'blind' person feels the shape then rests all or part of his body on the leader. The position is held for a short time for the 'blind' person to feel safe.

4 The leader then gradually changes the shape, moving a little way across the room but always keeping in contact with the 'blind' person and the process is repeated. The leader should try and alternate between low, middle and high shapes.

5 This continues until both have crossed the room. The pair swap roles to return.

A further variation on either of the above is for people to work in threes with two leaders, and one 'blind' person.

6 Some questions you might want to discuss:

How do you feel about what you have just done?

How did you feel as the blind person?

How did you feel as the leader?

What was easy/difficult?

What did you learn about the place/your leaders during the activity?

How do you think it looked?

Has the activity helped you in any way?

Comment: *There is a need for sensitivity towards those for whom physical contact, especially with members of the opposite sex, is unwelcome.*

"People with normal sight are often unaware of the difficulties partially sighted and blind people experience in their everyday lives. How could they? I feel that there are a number of things which would help. Firstly, if steps were all edged with white paint (I know that some are) there would be no problem. I think it would be a good idea to have a voice recorded timetable at underground stations. Also in the trains and buses a recording announcing the station or arrival of the vehicle at a stop would help."

*Moira Gladwish*

# P ACTIVITY 3 otatoes

## What are you doing now?

◊ In science, you may be investigating a natural object and want to develop observational skills.

◊ In geography, you might be studying a group of people in another country.

◊ You may be learning about other religions in RE.

## You might like to try C

You will need one potato for each member of the group and a largish bag or small sack to hold the potatoes.

**1** Sitting in a circle, give each person in the group a potato.

**2** Ask people to look carefully at their potato and really get to know it well.

**3** Collect all the potatoes in the bag, give it a shake then empty the potatoes out on to the floor or a table.

**4** Ask the group to pick out their own potato from the pile.

**5** Some questions you might want to discuss:

How easy/difficult was it to find your potato?

What made it easy/difficult?

What does this tell you about potatoes?

What can we learn from this about groups of people?

Comment: *Everyone invariably manages to find her or his own potato. What really needs to be brought out here is that within a group which shares certain characteristics that make them a group (in this case brown, roundish, knobbly) each individual is nonetheless unique, having qualities which mean it can be identified in a crowd. It is important to remember this when we are thinking about groups of people in different countries, with different belief systems and different cultural backgrounds from our own. (This same exercise is done with leaves in the section on Suffering and Joy (page 57) to emphasise the uniqueness of any part of creation.)*

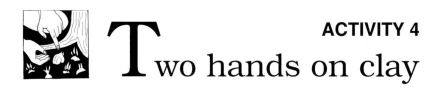

## ACTIVITY 4

# Two hands on clay

### What are you doing now?

◊ In science, you might be investigating different textures or the elasticity of a substance.

◊ You might be doing clay, plasticine or play-doh modelling in art.

◊ In language, you may be exploring vocabulary for describing textures and experiences without sight.

### You might like to try [C]

"My hands are part of my body and they are guided by my heart... My hands are my best friends; I like them very much, because I have a disability in my lower limbs. If I didn't have hands, I couldn't walk with crutches so I wouldn't walk at all. There are hands that start wars and others that make peace. But my hands will never start wars but they will make peace, they will love the people, the poor, and sick and that's how all the hands of the world should be."

*Cecilia*

You will need clay - enough for one lump between two, and a blindfold for each person in the group.

1 The group works in pairs who sit on opposite sides of a table where they can both reach the middle.

2 Each person is blindfolded, then a lump of clay is placed between them.

3 They are asked to touch the clay and to become aware of how it feels: the texture, temperature, weight, etc.

4 Together, in silence, they mould the clay into a shape.

5 The blindfolds are removed and the pairs view and discuss their work.

6 Individuals may wish to write about the experience.

7 Some questions you might want to discuss.

Does the shape look as you expected it to look?

How do you feel about the shape you created?

What was it like creating the shape with another person?

What did you find easy/difficult?

What connections can you make between this experience and others you, or people you know, have had?

How did you enjoy the activity?

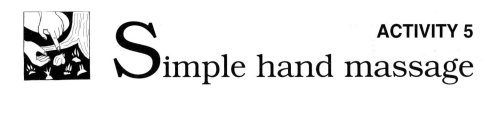

# Simple hand massage

## What are you doing now?

◊  You might be exploring relaxation techniques.

◊  You might be looking at feelings of wellbeing.

## You might like to try  C/A

You can massage the hand 'dry' or very lightly oiled.  The hands have a vast number of sensory nerves, so they are very receptive to massage.

Ask the children to get into pairs, a massager (A) and massagee (B). Read out the following instructions.

> Take B's hand gently, her palm facing down and supported underneath with the fingers of both your hands.  Use your thumbs to 'spread' the back of her hand open.

> Turn her hand over, resting it in one of your hands.  Make a loose fist with your other hand and make gentle circular movements with your knuckle all around the palm.

> Use both your hands to hold B's hand in the same position and use your thumbs to make tiny circles in the palm, covering the whole surface, then work from the wrist to the base of the fingers, pressing along imaginary lines with your thumbs.

> Still supporting her hand make the same tiny circular movements with your thumbs down the wrist from where the thumb ends.

> Turn B's hand over and support it at the wrist with one of your hands.  With the other, thumb above, index finger below, 'drain' between the bones of B's hand out towards the web between her fingers.

> Work along the side of each finger with your finger and thumb, ending at the fingertips.

> To finish, enclose B's hand in both your own and draw them very slowly along and off at her fingertips.

> Repeat the above on the other hand.

> End the massage by holding both B's hands and drawing them very slowly along and off at her fingertips.

> A and B then change roles.

"Study the hand, and you shall find in it the true picture of man, the story of human growth, the measure of the world's greatness and weakness."

*Helen Keller*

"A woman who was living an immoral life in the town had learned that Jesus was a guest in the Pharisees house and had brought oil of myrrh in a small flask.  She took her place behind him, by his feet, weeping.  His feet were wet with her tears and she wiped them with her hair, kissing them and anointing them with the myrrh."

*Luke 7:37*

When I was living in Sudan I finally began to understand some of those little things that had always puzzled me in the Bible. Why were they always putting oil on each other's feet? Now I knew. If you have been walking around in the burning hot sand in a pair of open shoes your feet become very dry and start to crack and get sore. You need to sit down and rub oil - ordinary cooking oil will do - into your feet or, better still, have someone else to do it for you.

SB

# ACTIVITY 6

# Picture a smell

## What are you doing now?

◊ In science you might be studying the body and its functions.

◊ You may be painting in an art lesson.

## You might like to try [C]

You will need a candle and a box of matches, a small bottle of aromatherapy oil, paints and a large sheet of paper for each person.

1 People sit in a circle and close their eyes.

2 A few drops of the oil are poured on the unlit candle, then it is lit and placed in the centre of the circle.

3 The group is asked to breathe in deeply and slowly and to concentrate on the smell.

4 Ask them, in silence, to think about the following questions:

> What colours does it remind you of?

> What shapes does it remind you of?

> What pictures come into your mind as you smell it?

5 After some minutes' reflection, bring the group gently back to awareness of their surroundings and ask them to paint what they have 'seen'.

6 In pairs, people discuss their pictures, then the main points are shared with the whole group.

7 Some questions you might want to discuss:

> What similarities are there between the pictures?

> What differences are there between the pictures?

> Why are there differences?

> How easy did you find the activity?

> Did you like the activity?

> Did anything surprise you?

> Will anything change as a result of this activity?

Comment: *Undiluted aromatherapy oils can be harmful. Check that the candles are extinguished before leaving the room. Do not leave the children during this activity.*

"If the doors of perception were cleansed, everything would appear to man as it is, infinite."

*William Blake*

 **ACTIVITY 7**

# A time to listen

## *What are you doing now?*

◊ You may be doing an activity where you want to still and centre the group.

◊ In RE you may be making time to listen to the sounds of creation.

## *You might like to try* C

1 The group sits in a circle and everyone makes themselves comfortable.

2 For a period of time (between one and five minutes depending on the age and maturity of the group) everyone sits in silence, with their eyes closed, breathes deeply and listens.

3 At the end of the time, gently remind the group of their surroundings and let them adjust before starting any discussion.

4 Some questions you might want to discuss:

What did you hear?

How did you feel?

Did anything surprise you?

Will this change anything for you?

Comment: *People may simply want to remain quiet and not discuss the exercise.*

"Waking up this morning, I smile. Twenty four new hours are before me. I vow to live fully in each moment and to look at all beings with eyes of compassion."

*Thich Nhat Hanh*

# ACTIVITY 8
# **M**usic improvisation

## *What are you doing now?*

◊   In music you may be experimenting with sounds.

◊   You may be creating a music and dance piece for a school concert or play.

## *You might like to try* | C |

As well as a large open room to work in you will need a large selection of things that make a noise: percussion instruments, bags that can be rustled and scrunched, building bricks to bang together, cans, spoons, boxes etc.

**1**   The group is split into two smaller groups: one group moves to the centre of the room (dancers) and the other goes to the 'instruments' (players).

**2**   The dancers sit down, close their eyes and listen.

**3**   The percussion group begins to play.  Anyone can play any instrument or make a sound by clapping or tapping part of his body.  The players choose their own rhythm, but may like to try and work together as they become more aware of the potential for sound.

**4**   The dancers keep their eyes closed and begin to make small movements to the sounds.  As they become more confident, they may wish to move out of their space or even get up and move around the room.

**5**   The groups swap over and repeat the process.

**6** Some questions you may want to discuss:

Which moments did the players enjoy watching most?

Which moments did the dancers enjoy most?

How did you feel as a player/dancer?

How did the fact that you could not see affect you?

Did the way you played/danced change as you grew more confident?

What was the most exciting moment?

What guided you in your playing/dancing?

What have you learned from this activity?

Comment: *The key to this activity is that the dancers cannot see what instruments are selected and therefore cannot anticipate the sound. They are relying totally on their hearing to guide them.*

Music does not have to be formal, on specially made instruments. When I lived in Sudan we would often be sitting on the verandah with neighbours when one would suddenly grab the metal bucket, turn it upside down and beat a rhythm on it. Others would get up and dance and we would all join in - just for the sheer fun of it.

SB

# T he missing ingredient

**ACTIVITY 9**

## *What are you doing now?*

◊ In science, you may be investigating combinations of foods, the principle of reactions or the idea of catalysts: that a little goes a long way.

◊ You may be eating school dinners.

## *You might like to try*

You will need the ingredients for any well-known, popular dish (potatoes might be a good way to start) and salt.

**1** Prepare the food without using salt.

**2** People taste some of the food and comment on the taste.

**3** Add a little salt.

**4** People taste the food again and comment on the taste.

**5** If possible, repeat the process with different dishes.

**6** Some questions you might like to discuss:

What is the difference between the two tastings?

How does salt change the taste?

What does this tell us about salt?

How much does salt affects the taste?

If there were no salt around, what changes would we have to make in our lives?

The same procedure could be used for other ingredients such as spices and herbs such as pepper and parsley.

Comment: *This is an activity about valuing an item that we tend to take for granted. The canteen staff may be able to help here, especially if the whole school is involved. For a set period of time, meals could be prepared without salt and the salt put on tables to be added later.*

*What is important here is that the change is qualitative. It is not about using a lot of salt, but about the fact that a very small quantity of salt changes the taste quite dramatically.*

"You are salt to the world. And if salt becomes tasteless, how is its saltness to be restored? It is good for nothing but to be thrown away and trodden underfoot."

*Matthew 5:13*

"Each stem is a flashing arrow, swift in the harvest.

Cane is sweet sweat slain,

cane is labour, unrecognised;

sugar is the sweet swollen pain of the years;

sugar is slavery's immovable stain...

Cane is a slaver;

cane is bitter, very bitter in the sweet blood of life."

*Faustin Charles*

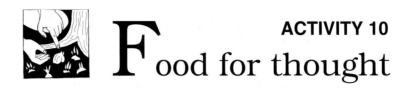

**ACTIVITY 10**

# Food for thought

## What are you doing now?

◊  In geography, you may be looking at exports and imports.

◊  You might be studying foods in science.

## You might like to try  C

You will need a piece of banana for each member of the group and a large sheet of paper and a pen.

**1**  People sit in a circle, close their eyes and relax.

**2**  Explain that you are going to give everyone a piece of fruit to eat and they are to think about, but not answer yet, the questions you ask them.

**3**  Each person is given a piece of banana to eat and as they eat, gently ask the following questions to guide their contemplation.

> Think about the taste in your mouth - what does it remind you of?... Think about the fruit... Where did it start its life?... What sort of weather did it have?... What sort of plant was its home?... What sort of things did it see every day?... What sounds did it hear?... How did it leave its plant?... How was it carried?... Where was it taken?... How did it come to us?... What was its journey like?... What sort of things did it see on its way?... What sort of sounds did it hear?... Where did it arrive?... How did it get from there to your mouth?... How does it end its life?... Can you still taste it?...
>
> Try and keep that taste with you as you open your eyes and come back to the classroom.

**4**  Brainstorm, without comment, the things the group experienced during their reflection on the taste of the banana.

**5**  Discuss any issues people may want to bring up as a result.

"Rosh Hashanah begins in the evening.  We get dressed in our best clothes.  We share a holiday dinner with our family and friends.  The hallah loaf is on the table.  Usually hallah is baked in a braid, but on Rosh Hashanah, it is round.  The round shape reminds us that one year is over and a new one is beginning.  We have come around in a circle.  We tear off a piece of the round golden hallah.  We dip it in honey to make it sweet.  We also eat pieces of apple dipped in honey.  Then we say, 'May the new year be sweet.'  We wish everyone a happy new year.  We say the Hebrew words, 'Shanah Tove, a good year.'  We send Rosh Hashanah cards to those who live far away."

# Cherishing opportunities for
# CELEBRATION
# & GRIEVING

"When you arise in the morning, give thanks for the morning light, for your life and strength. Give thanks for your food and the joy of living. If you see no reason for giving thanks, the fault lies in yourself."

*Tecumseh*

Celebration is about:

◊ making a song and dance about life; treating the day as something special

◊ recognising and experiencing gifts such as hope, joy, compassion, thankfulness, love and sorrow; and sorrow will be in there even as we celebrate.

Grieving is about:

◊ our response to our own and others' suffering; acceptance, letting go, finding peace.

◊ acknowledging anger and frustration.

Grieving and celebration are about:

◊ being fully present in the here and now with a heightened sensory awareness

◊ bringing together the past and the future into the present

◊ expressing the inexpressible and integrating that into ourselves; knowing that there is more to all this than meets the eye

◊ transformation.

Celebration and grieving may involve beauty through ritual and symbol, such as flowers and light, music, story, dance, blessing, shared food. They will usually be found in the everyday and be very simple and without any obvious symbol or ritual, but celebration can also be the outcome of long and careful planning.

Grieving is more often sudden and unexpected, but the likelihood is that, on any day, someone in your class or close to you is grieving. Encouraging children and staff in the school to understand and talk about their feelings may help them cope better with their emotions in times of sadness.

We would suggest that the activities here are not just used when a tragedy or happy event occurs but that discussion about sadness and grief and opportunities for celebration form part of everyday school life.

"Walk on a rainbow trail;
Walk on a trail of song,
and all about you will be beauty.

There is a way out of every dark mist,
over a rainbow trail."

*Navajo song*

# ACTIVITY 1

# The staff meeting

## *What are you doing now?*

◊ It may be that staff meetings feel a burden - yet another demand on your time.

◊ It may be that staff meetings seem full of business and busyness, but not much gets done.

## *You might like to try*  **A**

Arrange the chairs in a circle so that you can all see one another. You are all equally seen and heard in this circle, a symbol of unity.

Take a minute of quiet at the beginning of the meeting. A minute to become still and let go of some of the tension and busyness of the day can put us back in touch with ourselves.

Have a clear agenda - a 'story' of the meeting - and let it have a beginning, a middle and an end; let everyone be aware of that sense of purpose and progress, timing and pacing.

Use fable or poetry to express an idea that the staff is grappling with; it might inspire, raise questions, clarify or delight.

Celebrate the past - either ask each person to recall a moment of pleasure, delight or breakthrough that same day, or to look back since the last staff meeting and to recall what has gone well since then. Share as a group.

Let each person note what, right now, is their concern - where are they now?

Look at the business in hand, be it policy, making arrangements or a new resource, and then leave time to quietly reflect on it, before mulling it over together and discussing it.

Remember your vision, what it is you each and all really want to create, recall your purpose.

Close the meeting with celebration - perhaps each person saying what they take away from the meeting, what qualities they brought to the meeting.

"Don't be afraid to take a big step if one is indicated. You can't cross a chasm in two small jumps."

*D Lloyd George*

Comment: *There is no reason why staff meetings should not be enjoyable celebrations. Much more work and business gets done! Over the past ten years many inservice staff meetings have been held on the above basis. In it, there is the recognition that it is the people in the meeting, not just the papers, that are absolutely central. What matters is the experience they bring, it is their willingness to share, reflect, ponder, and make decisions in the light of their valued experience and vision. This has helped to make for energetic, productive staff meetings. The elements of celebration are there: symbol (the circle); treating it as a special time; becoming really present to the here and now; recalling the past; focusing on the future; becoming aware of things that matter, including hope and laughter. Flowers, music and candles can all bring pleasure or focus to a meeting.*

*It takes a little boldness at times to shift from the dreary and mundane to the celebratory. What if the other staff don't like it? What if it seems too different? What if it seems daft? There is a qualitative leap from the stodgy old business way to a celebration.*

# 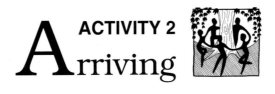ACTIVITY 2
# Arriving

## *What are you doing now?*

◊ It may be that at the beginning of the day it all feels a rush and rather bitty.

◊ It may be that at the beginning of the year children arrive in your form and things don't quite gel.

## *You might like to try* C

Have some music playing as the children come in.

Allow time for all to greet one another rather than just being ticked off on the register. A circle go-round would help here.

Have a clear programme for the day up on the wall - what is today all about? What's the purpose? Where are we going?

Make a time of quiet reflection for the children to think what it is they really want to achieve that day.

Read a brief story, fable or poem to raise questions, to find laughter.

Create a time for the children to share their news.

Have some flowers and plants around the room to use as objects for reflection and quiet activity.

Comment: *I have met teachers who treat their children like royal guests. They prepare for them as if they were the most important of people arriving. Shelagh would create as much beauty in the classroom as possible, with fabrics, colour, prints of great paintings. Walking into her classroom was like going into a special world - one that had been made ready to delight you. There were often surprises; the children would arrive and a whole new corner had appeared of stones and rocks and feathers. Beautiful music was playing as the first child arrived.*

"Poetry, fine art, music or any other creative field, we are all striving to bring beauty into our environment; that desire to create beautiful things stirs in every heart."

*W Taylor*

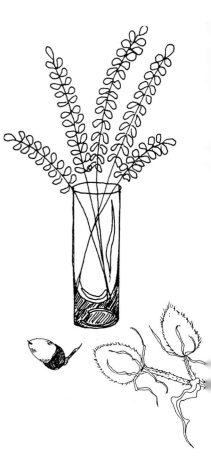

The first day of the year for Pete's children was fairly unforgettable. Days of work went into preparing for that first hour when the new J6 arrived. Each child had their place set out for them, their names carefully written, their books named and labelled, the room ready in every detail for them. A warm greeting from Pete and then off on a carefully prepared programme of activities beginning with a tape of Martin Luther King to invite the children to dream, to aspire to all that they may be.

# **W**elcoming ACTIVITY 3
## the newcomer

## *What are you doing now?*

◊   There may be traveller children who come for only a brief period to your school and who are not sure how they belong.

◊   Children from the Homeless Unit may come also for a brief period and may feel unsettled.

◊   There may be new staff, temporary staff, supply teachers or students, who have just arrived and are uncertain.

## *You might like to try* **C / A**

**1**   As a staff or as a class sit quietly and go back in your mind's eye to the times when you were a newcomer - perhaps when you moved house, changed jobs, began school etc.  Recall what it was like... What made it hard?  What made it pleasant?  How were you welcomed?  What really made you feel welcome and part of the place?

**2**   Open your eyes and jot down what you would want to make you feel really welcome next time you are the newcomer, the stranger.

**3**   Decide what you will do to ensure the next newcomer to the school is welcome.

**4**   Share with a partner.

Comment:  *Each newcomer is a cause for celebration.  How can we translate that celebration into practical steps?  This may require school policy decisions.*

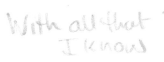

With all that
I know

Namaste

"With all the power of my arms,
With all the intelligence of my mind,
With all the love of my heart,
I pay my due respect to the soul -
Within you."

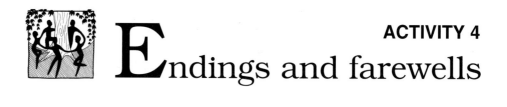

# Endings and farewells

*"You cannot stop the birds of sorrow from landing on your shoulder, but you can prevent them nesting in your hair."*

*Chinese proverb*

## What are you doing now?

◊ It may be the end of the year and your class is leaving.

◊ A staff member may be leaving.

## You might like to try  C/A

*"Grief is your friend.  It lets you mourn, remember, cry."*

*Fitz, in 'Cracker: the movie'*

1 Each person is given a blank page - an A4 sheet folded in two.

2 Look round the room at each person and think of something they have brought to you, taught you, over the last year.  What do you appreciate about each person?  What is the positive quality that makes them who they are?  Take time to reflect.

3 Pass the cards round.  On each person's card write what it is that you have gained from them, or what you appreciate about them.

4 Let each card go round to everyone before returning to its owner.

## Or you might try  C

1 As a class, brainstorm everything you have achieved in the year - reaching the high points and getting through the low spots.

2 In small groups work on producing posters; use words and images to celebrate the school year together.

3 Each group presents their posters to the class or school.

Comment:  *When a class has worked and played together for a year, it is well to mark the end.  If they are in the top junior class they will all be going in different directions.  With younger children some might be leaving.  As in any celebration there will be sadness as well as gladness - a recognition perhaps of what was not done, opportunities missed; a recognition of loss, knowing you will not all meet as one group again.*

# ACTIVITY 5
# Festivals

## What are you doing now?

◊ It may be that Christmas, Eid, Passover, Diwali, Holi or the other special times become very busy, full of activity and a little bit too full of stress and strain.

◊ Christmas may have become materialistic and a focus for getting and consuming goods.

◊ Issues of justice, peace and environmental responsibility may well disappear out of the window.

## You might like to try C/A [39]

1 Take time together to reflect on what the festival is all about for you - what it means to you.

2 Reflect on how the festival relates to the world today and to the issues of justice, peace and the environment.

3 Decide which elements of the festival you want to keep and be involved in and which you want to leave aside.

4 Think of who might feel excluded and how to involve them.

5 Enjoy the process as much as the product.

Comment: *Much has been written about Christmas, Eid, Passover, Diwali, Holi and the other special festivals. Each faith group will know what it is that it wants to communicate and these guidelines do not attempt that.*

*The festivals are, however, very relevant in the work on values and visions. Buried at the heart of the festivals are the themes of human existence, for example Passover celebrates freedom, justice and hope; Christmas celebrates incarnation, vulnerability and hope. All are times for the expression of community. Festivals are also times of suffering and exclusion. For all those who do not feel part of the community, the fun and pleasure of the celebration may well feel bitter and exclusive. The tradition within Passover to always invite the stranger to the meal is significant.*

"Play is essential to the life of the universe."

*Jackson and Killingly*

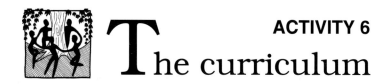

**ACTIVITY 6**

# The curriculum

## *What are you doing now?*

◊ You may be working on the curriculum, be it science, history, English.

◊ you may want more fun, joy and celebration to spring up all over the place.

"Suddenly from behind the rim of the moon, in long, slow-motion moments of immense majesty, there emerges a sparkling blue and white jewel, a light, delicate sky-blue sphere laced with slowly swirling veils of white, rising gradually like a small pearl in a thick sea of black mystery. It takes more than a moment to fully realise this is Earth... home."

*Edgar Mitchell, astronaut*

## *You might like to try* C

In English, ask groups to look through the newspapers for any items of good news. Choose the most important item. Each group is to find a way of presenting it creatively through report, story, poem etc. in the school assembly. Use music, flowers and light to make it a very celebratory 'Good News' assembly.

In history, draw a time line up to the present and place on it any people throughout history who have made a positive difference. Create poems/pictures to celebrate those lives and keep them up and around the classroom.

In geography, look at a disaster such as a cyclone (See 'News from Pallem' in the section on Suffering and Joy, page 71) and find out what good came out of it. [40]

In science use reflection, contemplation, visioning to get in touch with the wonder of creation (see 'The leaf' in the section on Suffering and Joy on page 60). Use an earth walk [12] to explore textures, colours, sounds. Use the poems of Gerard Manley Hopkins to delight and heighten our observation. Work on the body, on light, power, matter, the earth in space, nature are all areas for celebration. [41]

Comment: *The good news and wonder in these subjects will be shallow unless grounded in a whole school ethos which takes on board suffering as well as celebration.*

*Celebration breaks free of management. All the most carefully laid plans cannot in themselves create celebration. It can be perhaps the most wondrous and awesome of events. It brings together aspects of all the other sections in these guidelines - a sense of self, a coming together in the community, an enjoyment of creation, openness to suffering and joy, encounter, listening, story, reflection and contemplation, heightened sensory awareness, visioning and a sense of purpose and commitment to action. If there truly has been celebration we are changed and will never be quite the same again. It may be at a meal shared, an encounter, a moment of wonder, a new understanding.*

Having listened to the story of the Passover, having encountered the Jewish man who shared his story and vision with us during this activity, one teacher said: "I do not know what of this I will take back to the classroom, but I know that I am changed so everything I do now will have been changed."

In listening to the Passover story the teachers said that they had felt a sense of continuity, an awareness of something that is eternal; they touched on themes relevant for us today, themes that always remain - slavery or freedom; they sensed the complexity of life and how, within the celebration, there was yet sorrow.

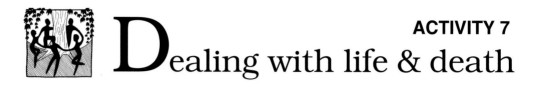

# Dealing with life & death

## What are you doing now?

◊ You may be dealing with life and death in RE.

◊ You may have a tragedy to face in the school community.

◊ You may become involved in discussion with the class following a disaster or the death of a well-known person.

## You might like to try  C

1 Create a safe place where the children can talk openly and in confidence about their thoughts and experiences of life and death: of family, friends, famous people or pets. There needs to be ample time to deal with and debrief the issues raised. The children will hopefully be able to leave feeling that they have been listened to. Sensitivity needs to be used at all times. In a case of tragedy affecting the school community or individuals, it may be appropriate to seek assistance and support from professional counsellors.

2 Help the children to express sadness in their lives through talking, drawing, painting, clay modelling, writing, movement or music.

3 Explore life cycles in the natural world using activities from Sharing Nature with Children [11], or similar books which encourage empathy and interconnectedness with the created world.

4 Explore what happens in different cultures after someone dies. Look at mourning and expressions of grief, ritual and customs, memorials and celebrations, life cycles and interconnectedness.

---

*My feelings*

I feel sad. Inside me I think I am going to burst. My Nan has had a stroke. I cant really tell anyone because I would cry. She is getting better but it is impossible for her to get better completely. I am really hoping that she will see through Christmas. I am going to try and get her something really nice for Christmas. She is very old and I suppose it would be kinder for her to be in peace with God.

Sara Liles

---

"Since every death diminishes us a little, we grieve - not so much for the death as for ourselves."

*Lynne Caine*

A Manchester school for severely disabled children has a well thought-out approach to handling the death of children from the school, which combines careful, loving and thoughtful consideration of the memory of the child and the celebration of their life:

"When the staff discover that one of the children has died, a candle is lit in the classroom as a sign for all the children who may or may not have any language.

"Those who can, share the good things they remember about the dead child, and look at the many photographs the school always keeps of each child. There will be things in the classroom which remind everyone of the friend who has died and these are shared, discussed and looked at. As the children gain in maturity and understanding they are encouraged to share in the celebration of the dead child's life."

This caring school has provided many teachers with a model to consider for their own school to enable them to deal with a difficult situation with great sensitivity.

My mother has experienced four sudden deaths in her life: both parents, her husband and a close aunt. 'You're allowed a certain time to grieve,' she says, 'about three or six months, then everybody starts telling you to pull yourself together and to get on with life. It's not like that. You can't just switch off grief.'

SB

## ACTIVITY 8

# Developing empathy

### What are you doing now?

◊ You may be involved in discussion with the class following a disaster.

◊ The children may be talking about a well-known person who has died.

◊ In the playground, the children may be playing shooting or war games.

### You might like to try C

1 Discuss the disaster or the death, focusing on the place and the situation.

2 In groups or as a class (as appropriate) create a frozen tableau of the scene of death.

3 Each person in the tableau thinks of one word to express his feelings. At a given signal everyone shouts out that word.

4 "Defrost" individuals in the scene to discuss how they are feeling there and then.

5 Role play supporting a close relative or friend of the dead person.

6 As a group/class discuss what happens next: the next day, the next few days, the next week, the next month, a year later. How long does grief last?

# Using VISIONING

Visioning is about:

◊ using our imagination

◊ creating and exploring images to look at the present, to return to the past and most significantly to visit the future

◊ allowing images to come to mind, valuing those images and responding to them

◊ the ordinary and everyday, the local and the global.

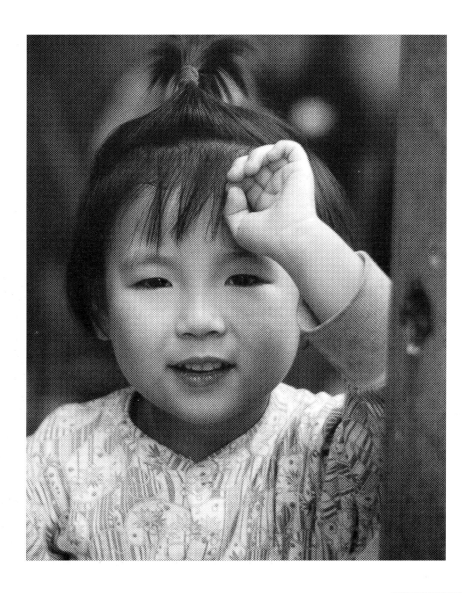

One of our most powerful tools in creating something is our imagination. When we set out to do something, create something, we need to know where we are going. Quite literally we need to know/ visit that place to which we are going; we can visit it with our imagination. It is not surprising that prophets, in their concern to invite people to another and a better way of living, have always evoked images of how the world may be. They have also been open to receiving images and visions [42]. If we are working on spiritual development one aspect of work will be vision.

It is not simply prophets who have vision. All people have it. In *Values and Visions* the importance of each person's vision is affirmed as being something that shapes their lives and their world.

In this section we will look at a few activities to enjoy the present, to explore concepts such as justice, peace and creation in specific terms, to envision change at the local and global level and to help set realisable goals.

Some visioning will be very simple indeed and will happen there and then on the spot. For example a staff member says they want to see more parents involved in the school. Ask them "What would it look like? What would they be doing?" Give them a moment to reflect, to close their eyes and literally imagine parents being involved. Other visioning work will be a little more complex. It might involve a guided fantasy as in some of the following activities. Before using a guided fantasy it is often a good idea to encourage people to relax and focus. This will usually involve asking them to become aware of their breathing and to focus just on that. [43]

The power of imagination is immense. Let's harness it.

"I say to you today, my friends, that in spite of the difficulties and frustrations of the moment, I still have a dream.

I have a dream that one day this nation will rise up and live out the true meaning of its creed. We hold these truths to be self-evident: that all men are created equal.

I have a dream that one day little black boys and black girls will be able to join hands with little white boys and white girls and walk together as brothers and sisters.

I have the audacity to believe that peoples everywhere can have three meals a day for their bodies, education and culture for their minds, and dignity, equality and freedom for their spirits. I believe that what self-centred men have torn down, other-centred men can build up.

I don't know what will happen now. We've got some difficult days ahead. But it doesn't matter with me now, because I've been to the mountain top. And I don't mind. Like anybody, I would like to live a long life; longevity has its place. But I'm not concerned about that now. I just want to do God's will. And He's allowed me to go up to the mountain. And I've looked over. And I've seen the promised land. I may not go there with you. But I want you to know tonight that we as a people will get to the promised land."

*Martin Luther King, Jr*

# **W**ACTIVITY 1 **W**aterfall

## *What are you doing now?*

◊ You may be helping a class to be calm and refreshed.

◊ You may be doing a project on light.

◊ You may be preparing to do some RE work on 'self'.

## *You might like to try*  **C**

**1** Ask the children to make themselves comfortable and gently close their eyes, take a few moments to relax and to become aware of their breathing.

**2** When everyone appears to be settled, read the following. Take your time and give the children time to imagine as you go along:

> With each breath let your body become more and more relaxed. With each out breath breathe out any worry... with each in breath feel yourself breathing in quietness and calm...

> Now imagine a beautiful waterfall of light entering the top of your head... Feel the waterfall of light gently flowing through your head... down your neck... into your chest and shoulders... The waterfall of light is warm and full of gentle energy... Feel it move down from your shoulders, into your arms... your hands and out through your fingers. More light falls as a waterfall down your back - into your tummy - your legs - down to your feet and out through your toes - washing away with it any stress or worry.

> Now you are completely bathed in a continuous waterfall of light... enjoy its freshness and the gentle calm it brings... in a moment you are going to leave the waterfall of light and you will find yourself back in the classroom, relaxed and refreshed. When you are ready open your eyes and stretch.

Comment: *The purpose of this activity is to create a moment of peace for the children. Many come from homes which are busy and noisy, to schools that are also busy and noisy. If children are to value peace they will need to explore some of its many facets including that of refreshment and calm.* [44]

"Say no to peace
If what they mean by peace
is the quiet misery of hunger,
the frozen stillness of fear,
the silence of broken spirits,
the unborn hopes of the
oppressed.

Tell them that peace is the
shouting of children at play,
the babble of tongues set free,
the thunder of dancing,
and a father's voice singing."

*from a poem by Brian Wren in
Bread of Tomorrow*

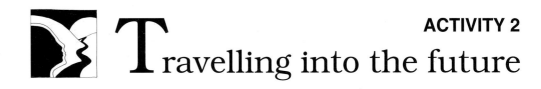

# Travelling into the future

## *What are you doing now?*

◊ You may be working on environmental science.

◊ In RE you may be exploring the idea of community.

◊ You might be preparing for creative writing.

◊ You might be working on a topic such as housing, homelessness, transport or work.

## *You might like to try*

1 Ask the children to sit comfortably; to close their eyes and take a few moments to relax; to become aware of their breathing flowing in and flowing out.

2 Read the following text to the children:

> Imagine that you are somewhere very peaceful... You look up and you see a time machine in front of you... Walk up to it... What can you see?... Touch it - what does it feel like?... Notice its shape...

> You climb into the machine... and you see the controls... On the control board the arrow is pointing to the year 2040, about 50 years from now. You press the control and as you do so you feel yourself and the time machine being gently yet swiftly lifted up and carried off into the future... As you move, you see light moving around you...

> You are now arriving at the year 2040... Feel the machine landing gently... Now you are getting out of the machine and onto the land and it is the year 2040. Take a first look around - what can you see?... what can you hear?... what does it feel like to be here?...

> See the people living here... Speak with them... Find out what their family life is like... what they eat... how they live... what music they enjoy... what work they do... what art they like...Have a look at what they are doing... at their faces... Visit where they live... Look at the environment... What is growing there? Take a good look round... What can you see?... What can you hear...? Perhaps there is one person you want to spend some time with. Do that now...

> Now you have a few minutes to look around at whatever you want...

(After two minutes) It is time to leave now so return to your time machine. As you climb into it take a last look... What was the most important thing that you have seen in this visit to the future?

And now you are about to leave. Set the control to 'time present' and return safely to this room... When you are ready open your eyes and stretch and you will find yourself back here in the classroom.

3  Write down or draw what you saw.

4  Get into pairs and talk about it.

5  If there is anything you particularly liked/disliked in the year 2040, share it with the whole class.

6  Talk about and list as a class some of the elements you want there to be in your world in the future.

7  Is there anything you can do now to create that future?

8  Make a class mural of the future.

Comment: *This activity can be adapted to focus on any aspect the class might be working on - to take a look at future possibilities in how communities organise themselves. The emphasis can be varied and might be housing and homelessness, food and famine or transport and pollution.*

*The time machine can of course also be used to go back in time, to visit a specific historical time. For instance, if you are working on explorers and encounters [45] you could use this to look at what it must have felt like for the Caribs and the Tainos and the other people of what became known here as the New World. This takes us into the area of suffering.*

# Mental maps
## of the playground

**ACTIVITY 3**

### *What are you doing now?*

◊   You may be doing design and technology.

◊   You may be tackling the issue of bullying.

### *You might like to try* C/A

You will need big sheets of sugar paper, enough felt tips, pastels and small pieces of card for everyone in the class.

**1**   Get into groups of three.

**2**   Now close your eyes and let yourself imagine the school playground.  Imagine it as an ideal school playground where everything is peaceful.

**3**   Open your eyes and together draw a mental map of a peaceful playground.  A mental map is any drawing of images, symbols, words that show what you had in your mind's eye. [46]

**4**   Share with another group.  Find and note down elements that you have in common.

**5**   Repeat each stage of the above activity but this time imagine a school playground where there is a lot of conflict and bother.

**6**   As a class, gather in the elements of the peaceful and the conflict-filled playground.

**7**   Some questions you might like to discuss:

How did the boys and girls relate in each playground?

How did the teachers and children relate?

How did the lunchtime organiser and children relate?

How was the playground shared?

Were there rules?

If so what were they?

Who made them?

What did you like/dislike about each playground?

How did people get on with one another?

How does your playground resemble the mental maps?

How do you want your playground to be?

**8** Brainstorm as a class possible action to create the playground you want.

**9** Decide individually what you will do to make the playground a better place to be.

**10** Share with a partner.

**11** Jot your resolve down on a card and have a look at it at the end of term.

**12** Review progress periodically.

Comment: *This activity has been used for two decades with countless children and teachers. Two of the themes which have constantly emerged are racism and sexism. In a school which is unwilling to challenge the barriers of negativity caused by racism and sexism, the consequences of those barriers will often be acted out in the playground. Work on something like the playground demands more than the goodwill of the children; it requires policy and structures within the school.[47] An individual boy may resolve to get in fewer fights but if the absence of a gender policy leaves sexism busily creating divisions in the school, his individual efforts will be unsupported.*

*Moreover, in many schools there is racism and this erupts in the playground, safe out of teacher earshot. It is, therefore, important if working with children on issues in the playground to ask the staff, including lunchtime organisers and governors, to consider the policy implications of a peaceful playground atmosphere.[48]*

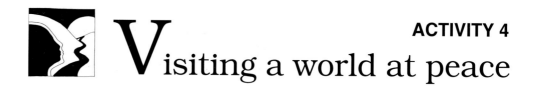 **ACTIVITY 4**

# Visiting a world at peace

## What are you doing now?

◊ You may be doing RE on 'getting on with others'.

◊ You may be beginning the school year with a new class and you may want to know about their values and visions at the outset.

> "A map without Utopia on it, it has been said, is not worth consulting... Admittedly there are disadvantages in dreams and ideals, the disadvantages of unreality and abstractions. But frequently it also clears and strengthens your mind if you venture to dream for a while, as concretely and as practically as possible, about the ideal situation to which all your current efforts are, you hope, directed."
>
> *Robin Richardson*

## You might like to try

**1** Use either a guided fantasy as in Activity 2 on page 168 or use reflection and a mental map as in Activity 3 on page 170.

**2** Some questions you might like to discuss:

What is it like there?

What are the people like?

How do people get on with one another?

What sort of work is going on?

How do people work?

How are resources shared?

How do people enjoy themselves?

In what ways is it a multicultural world?

Where are you in this world?

What aspects of it do you particularly like/dislike?

In what ways does it resemble our world/school?

> "Whatever you can do, or dream you can, begin it.
>
> Boldness has genius, power and magic in it."
>
> *Goethe*

Comment: *The theme could be varied to visit a world where there is enough for all.[49] Children inevitably have a vision of the future.[50] For many it is a bleak one, it may be one without hope. It may well be based on a harsh present and the belief that the future will be little different. A surprising number of children interviewed [51] believe not only that their own futures are bleak but also that the survival of the planet itself is uncertain. For children to carry this hopelessness silently around with them is hard. It may be expressed in a myriad of ways - lack of interest, lack of enthusiasm, destructiveness etc. Use of guided fantasy can encourage children to dream and to hope. Curiously enough fantasies often turn out to be highly practical; after all the imagination tends only to see what it has already seen in some form. The fantasies usually come up with a lot of specific detail of things seen and heard.[52] If we are working on spiritual development it is crucial that we offer children opportunities to dream and to hope; to know that the world may indeed be other than it is. Grounding that hope in reality is also essential.[53]*

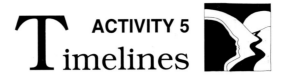

# ACTIVITY 5
# Timelines

## What are you doing now?

◊ You may be working on a topic such as homes and homelessness, water or food.

## You might like to try C

"First say to yourself what you would be; and then do what you have to do."

*Epictetus*

1 As a class brainstorm everything about the topic of Housing and Homes [54] now, in the present day.

2 Look at a wide selection of photos of homes [55] here and elsewhere in the world and add to the initial brainstorm. You may wish to have extra information about homelessness. [56]

3 Reflect quietly for a few minutes on how you want it to be in the year 2040. What sort of homes will there be? Will there be homes for everyone? Imagine the ideal future with respect to homes.

4 Now individually draw a timeline, starting from birth and going into the future. One line represents your life until now; one is for the probable future and one is for an ideal future.

5 Share your timelines with someone else and decide what are the most important ideas on your lines.

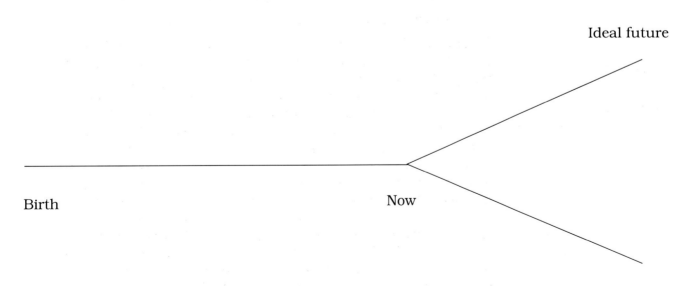

A timeline

**6** Some questions you might like to discuss:

> What is the difference between the future lines you have drawn?

> How did you decide which things to put on which line?

> Which of your suggestions is the easiest to do? Why?

> Which of your suggestions is the most difficult to do? Why?

**7** Draw up a class poster that shows with images and words the sort of future housing you as a class want to see in your village/town/city/country/world. [57]

**8** You may want to invite someone from the housing department to come in and talk with you and answer your questions. Likewise, you may want to talk with someone from one of many organisations working on homelessness. [58]

A variation on this timeline activity is Personal Timelines, where people plot their own life history from the day they were born till now along the line, then reflect on their own futures. An example of this is shown below.

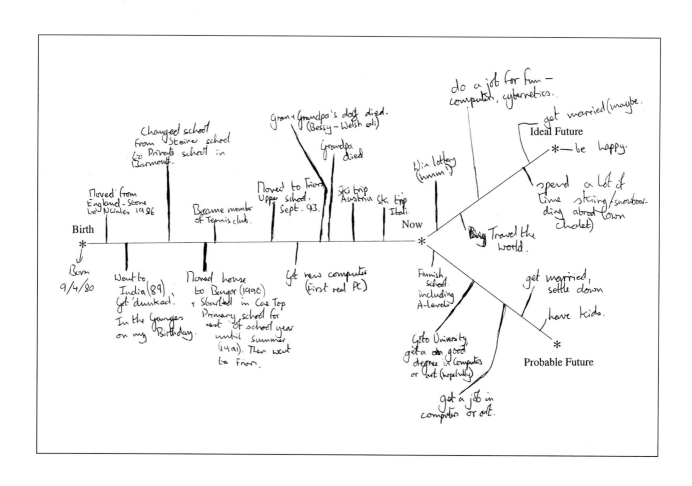

# $S$etting goals

ACTIVITY 6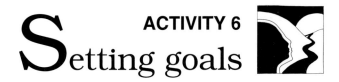

## What are you doing now?

◊ You may be planning a piece of work as a teacher.

◊ As a whole staff you may be undertaking an initiative.

◊ Children in your class may be planning a project.

## You might like to try

1 Choose your goal. To begin with, choose one which is fairly easy for you to believe in, that you feel is possible to realise in the fairly near future. (Later, take on more challenging ones).

2 Create a picture in your mind of the situation exactly as you want it. Think of it in the present tense as already existing the way you want it. Include as much detail as possible.

3 Jot down the key elements of your mental picture and in the course of working towards your goal look every now and then at the key elements and remember to visualise the goal. "What does it look like?".

Comment: *Images, like words, are powerful and can create an internal landscape that strengthens us, bringing clarity and confidence. Our logical left brain will have little time for this approach and may well think it ridiculous. However, the combination of using left brain logic and right brain imagery has proved to be an effective and creative way of working.* [59]

# Down to earth

## *What are you doing now?*

◊ You may be working with colleagues to develop an RE or environmental programme for your school.

NB: It is important to do this exercise in context, and not to do it 'cold'!

## *You might like to try*  **A**

This is a meditation about the web of life. It is about experiencing ourselves as rooted in the earth and connected to the whole of the web of life.[60]

**1** Read the following out loud:

> Make yourself comfortable and take a few moments to relax and to become aware of your breathing... With each out breath, breathe out any tension in your body... Allow the tension to dissolve as the breath goes out... Feel the breath filling your lungs... Allow the breathing to happen and allow the life-giving air to flow into you, to nourish and sustain you... The air you breathe is shared by the others in the room... The breath in your lungs now was a few moments ago the breath that was in your neighbour's lungs... Yesterday it may have been in the lungs of someone miles away... The air you breathe in now may be the air that was breathed out last week by a Bosnian refugee, by a hungry child in Somalia, by a soldier in Iraq, by a woman in Chernobyl... This air sustains life in all of us, the gift of life which none of us has earned.
>
> Imagine the air entering your lungs... See the oxygen being drawn into your bloodstream... Become aware of the energy that it brings... tiny explosions of energy... Picture the thousand tiny explosions of life-giving energy happening each second in your lungs. See the energy as points of light... linking up and becoming streams of light... circulating in the bloodstream and being carried into every part of your body... bringing you the gift of life moment by moment.
>
> See the threads of energy and light as fine filaments stretching out from your body... forming an aura... intersecting with the aura of those around you... Together these filaments form a delicate web of light... of energy... Through the web you are linked to those around you... to the

people with whom you work... to men and women and children several miles from here... to people far away in Africa, Asia, Latin America. The web carries love and care... it carries pain and loss... hope and joy. Open yourself up to being part of this web of life.

This web of life is not just made up of spiritual energy; it is made up of the stuff of the earth... electrical impulses, light waves, gravity... all the interactions of atoms and molecules...and the emanations given off by every living thing... The web links you to animals, for they are made of the same stuff as you... they breathe the same air as you... The milk that you drank this morning came from moist grass eaten by the cow... Its body has nourished yours.

The web of life links you to the plants... The bread that you ate this morning was made of the wheat which drew moisture and nourishment from the earth. It grew and ripened in the sun... it was harvested, ground and baked... It brings you minerals from the earth and energy from the sun... And when the time comes you will give back your body to the earth, to provide nourishment for other living beings which in turn give back their life to continue the cycle of life...

The web of life existed before you... you were born into it. It extends back through time, linking you to your mother and father, your grandparents... and their grandmothers and grandfathers... Back through hundreds and thousands of years... the web has never been broken... it goes back to the first communities of humans who came to this land... back to the very first women and men, and back beyond them to our remote ancestors in the trees... and back beyond them to the creatures that first crawled out of the sea... to the very earliest forms of life... The web links us to all these creatures that share with us the bounty of the one earth that has nourished us all.

"Who are we, and why are we on this earth? We turn to the creation to guide us, to give us the answer to what path we will take. We seek and value vision in our lives."

*Positive Indian Parenting*

"To see a World in a grain of sand, and a Heaven in a wild flower,

Hold Infinity in the palm of your hand, and Eternity in an hour."

*William Blake*

Now glide forward along the web... become aware of yourself now as absolutely unique... bearing a genetic heritage that is the legacy of millions of years. Allow yourself to appreciate that you have been given your own completely unique place in the web of the world... in the web of life.

Open yourself once again to the energies flowing in the web... the light... the excitement... the creativity constantly at work. And be open also to the pain that comes along the strands of the web... For if you are shutting out the pain you are shutting out the life... Allow yourself to grieve with the mother in Somalia whose child has starved to death, with the child who has lost her father through war in Mozambique, with the people of the forests as their forests are destroyed.

We have been born into this web and are here at this critical time... We can be a source of hope... This is a dark time... a time of fear... a time to face the darkness and to reach out beyond it in confidence of new life... For we do not face the darkness alone... We are part of the web and from it we draw strength... We give ourselves into it and allow ourselves to be nourished and sustained by it... We allow ourselves to be led into the future...

Still sensing our connection one with another and with the web of life, we return to this room... stretch... and when we feel ready, slowly open our eyes.

**2** Quietly reflect on the meditation and when ready share with another anything that particularly struck you.

Comment: *Our physical rootedness in the earth is a fact that we have generally lost sight of. It is something that for many peoples is essential to their understanding of who they are in the world. This activity begins to help us to experience our physical connectedness to one another and to the earth. If the issues of justice, peace and the integrity of creation are to mean anything to us we need to know ourselves as being connected to them through our being part of creation.*

I HAVE SPREAD MY DREAMS UNDER YOUR FEET;
TREAD SOFTLY. YEATS

# PART III

# PURPOSE and ACTION

# PURPOSE & ACTION

Purpose and action is about:

◊ how we treat one another

◊ how we meet one another's needs

◊ what we do or do not do, not what we say

◊ making a difference and creating 'bit by bit a more perfect world'. [61]

*"Is this the kind of fast that I require,*
*a day of mortification such as this;*
*That a person should bow his head like a bulrush*
*and use sackcloth and ashes for a bed?*
*Is that what you call a fast,*
*a day acceptable to the Lord?*

*Rather, is not this the fast I require:*
*to loose the fetters of injustice,*
*to untie the knots of the yoke,*
*and set free those who are oppressed,*
*tearing off every yoke?*
*Is it not sharing your food with the hungry,*
*taking the homeless poor into your house,*
*clothing the naked when you meet them,*
*and never evading a duty to your kinsfolk?*
*Then your light will break forth like the dawn."*

Isaiah 58: 5-7

This passage points out that a spirituality that does not express itself effectively in responding to needs for freedom, justice and the basics of food and housing is really a tiresome and empty spirituality. Schools have enough to weary them without that sort of spirituality.

Action is related to contemplation and vision. It is the embodiment of the decision to act or not to act. Having reflected on a particular issue, we may decide that we need to act, to do something (write a letter of protest, make something, give something), or that we need not to act, not to do something (not eat meat, not buy food from a particular place, not use a car).

In this section we look at a few quite simple activities that can make a difference in school and in the wider community. A number of them draw on Jewish teachings, but action relates to those of all faiths and of no faith.

Action without reflection and contemplation is just busyness. Action without vision has no context or future. Mindful action will be rooted in our reflection on the past and the present and it will be able to grow up into the space provided by vision. Ideally action is the outward expression of our inner understanding, values and visions. It is about getting on and creating what we say and what we want as individuals and as a community. The action for justice, peace and the environment taken within the school embodies the action that may be taken in the wider world.

In this section we shall look at:

◊ a few simple activities that can make a difference in school and in the wider community

◊ how action relates to reflection and contemplation and vision

◊ how this area of action relates to those of all faiths and of no faith.

# Generating class rules

## What are you doing now?

◊   You may be beginning a new year with a new class.

*"Teachers open the door, but you must enter by yourself."*

*Chinese proverb*

## You might like to try  C/A

1   At the end of the first week, after the children have begun to know you and one another, ask them to brainstorm as a class what are the sorts of things they want for their classroom.  How do they want their classroom to be?

2   Ask them then to brainstorm the rules they would need for the classroom they want.

3   Ask them in pairs or threes to choose their 'top three' rules - and to reach a consensus on that choice.

4   Ask them to present to the class their choice and to explain why they chose those rules.

Each year a J6 class in a Wigan school draws up its rules.  This is not the first task of the term but comes at the end of a rich and full first week.  They have had the opportunity to listen to Martin Luther King, to choose and explore stories, to think about and share out class responsibilities, to get stuck in on the theme for the term and to get to grips with basics; they have heard poems and fables that reach into the questions of race and gender.  Then out of that experience of the first week of working together they draw up their rules.  There is a remarkable hum of activity and quiet sense of contentment and responsibility in that classroom.

*"If only I could so live and so serve the world that after me there should never again be birds in cages..."*

*Isak Dinesen*

**5** List as a whole class all the 'top three' rules. Are there any missing? Are there any that someone disagrees with?

**6** Ask them to take a few minutes to look through the rules quietly and to talk about them in their twos and threes.

**7** Are there any changes they want to make? Are they all happy with them?

**8** If and when there is a general consensus ask two people to work on producing the Classroom Rules (or Charter). They may want to put them on computer or they may want to use calligraphy and art work.

**9** When the rules have been drawn up, one child presents them to the whole class for adoption.

**10** Place the chart somewhere visible where everyone can refer to it.

"Truly I say to you, unless you turn and become like children, you will never enter the kingdom of heaven."

*Matthew 18:2*

*Our rules by J6C*

*Work quietly*

*Do more work*

*Keep the classroom tidy*

*Be kind*

*Work as a team*

*Equal opportunities*

*Listen*

*Be sensible*

*Look after everything*

*Ask before taking*

*Be careful*

*Share things*

*Solve problems by talking*

*Show respect to other people*

*Help people*

*Be honest*

Comment: *The rules this class adopted for themselves get regularly used. At the end of the week review they considered what had not gone well. (See the section on Community, page 21). Their suggestion for dealing with this was 'refer to class rules'.*

*The class rules generated by children, if applied to the global community, would make a remarkable difference. In setting them and using them in school the children are creating a model of how it might be in the wider world. Just imagine if nations asked before taking.*

# ACTIVITY 2
# Gathering information

## and passing it on

## *What are you doing now?*

◊ You may be doing geography, media work, environmental science.

◊ You may be preparing an assembly.

## *You might like to try*  **C**

1 Ask the children to work in pairs or groups to gather information about the topic in hand, be it the issue of water, Bosnia, homes and homelessness, food and famine. Brainstorm all the possible sources of information - people, radio, TV, newspapers, books etc.

2 Ask them to select the five most 'important' pieces of information. (Let them set the criteria for what is important.)

3 Ask them to think of the best way to share that information with the rest of the class or the school. They might like to make posters, give a report, present a short drama, write a poem etc.

Comment: *We sometimes think that 'doing' is simply making or giving. But sometimes action is very low key and yet no less important. Gathering information and passing it on is a vital part in the whole spectrum of activity. (See Alemitu's story in Suffering and Joy, page 66). In a school in Wigan one form undertook a project on environmental responsibility. Much of this work involved gathering information and then telling other classes about it. As 'Earthkeepers' they spoke passionately for the earth - the other children listened very attentively.*

"In terms of modern social justice the Holocaust holds a hugely important lesson for everyone - the devastating power of the sin of silence. For Jews especially this places an obligation to speak out against injustices of all - even when we are told 'it is none our business'."

*Steve Miller*

# ACTIVITY 3
# Tzedakah

## What are you doing now?

◊ You may be looking at Judaism as part of a project on other religions.

◊ You may be wishing to link your classroom fundraising to wider values and issues.

## You might like to try ⟨C⟩

Tzedakah is a Hebrew word meaning the right things to do, the just thing, what people do for each other because that's what people ought to do for each other. Tzedakah is a basic Jewish value referring specifically to giving one's money away to those in need, 10 to 20 per cent of one's income being the recommended amount. It can also carry the additional connotation of any form of giving: time, money, effort, energy, talents to make a more just world. It is the obligation of every Jew to give Tzedakah - to perform an act of justice by helping those in need, not out of a feeling of pity but out of religious duty. In a sense Tzedakah is Judaism's life force. It is an idea made real that points to hope, trust, faith and much more. It is a mode of behaviour that brings life to those who may have been downtrodden or defeated, energising those who have been weary to their bones and to their soul.[61]

1  Reflect with the children on where there is need in the world. What concerns them? Reach an agreement on what concerns them most.[62]

2  Tell one of these two Jewish stories about Tzedakah:

Story 1: [63]

In the 16th century a famous Rabbi, Isaac Luria, observed that in his world, like ours, many things seemed to be wrong. "How could God allow such terrible things to happen?" wondered Luria. "Perhaps," he suggested, "it is because God needs our help." He explained his answer with a story about the time before the world was created. "When first setting out to make the world, God planned to pour a holy light into everything to make it real. God made special containers to hold the holy light. But the light was just too much for the containers to hold and they burst, shattering into millions of broken pieces like dishes dropped onto the floor." Our world is a mess because it is filled with broken fragments. That is why God created us and gave us the freedom of choice. We are free to do whatever we please with

"An Innu hunter's prestige comes not from the wealth he accumulates but from what he gives away. When a hunter kills caribou or other game he shares with everyone else in the camp."

*Daniel Ashini*

"Let every word be the fruit of action and reflection. Reflection alone without action or tending towards it is mere theory, adding its weight when we are overloaded with it already... Action alone without reflection is being busy pointlessly. Honour the word eternal and speak to make a new world possible."

*Helder Camara*

our world. We can allow things to remain broken or, as Luria urged, we can try to repair the mess. Luria's Hebrew phrase for 'repairing the world' is tikun olam.

## Story 2: [63]

One day a rich baker was sleeping in the synagogue. As he was half dozing the biblical verses telling the children of Israel to place twelve loaves in the tabernacle were being read (Leviticus 24:5-6). In his sleepy state he thought that it was God who had spoken to him directly. He wasn't sure why God would need bread but he was proud to be asked and rushed home to bake the bread. When he came back to the synagogue he tucked the loaves behind the curtain next to the scrolls of the Bible. No sooner had he gone than the poorest man in the village, the synagogue cleaner, came into the sanctuary. All alone he whispered his prayer, "O Lord. I am so poor. My family is starving. We will die unless you perform a miracle for us." He then walked around the room to tidy it up. As he approached the scrolls he saw the loaves of bread. "A miracle!" he exclaimed. "I never thought you worked so quickly!" Minutes later the baker returned, curious as to what had happened. He was amazed. "You really ate my bread, Lord! I will bring you more next week." And he did, and this strange exchange continued for many years until the rabbi by chance was in the synagogue late one day and saw what happened. He called the two men together and told them what they had been doing. "I see," said the baker sadly, "God doesn't really eat bread." "I understand," said the poor man, "God hasn't been baking bread for me after all." They were both sad that God would no longer be a part of their lives. Then the rabbi said, "Look at your hands. Your hands," he said to the rich man, "are the hands of God giving food to the poor. And your hands," he said to the poor man, "are also the hands of God receiving gifts from the rich. So continue baking and continue taking. Your hands are the hands of God."

3 Explain the Jewish concept of Tzedakah as justice rather than charity, by using the texts in these guidelines. Ask a representative of a local Jewish community to come into your class or contact Tzedek (see the address list).

4 The great Jewish teacher Moses Maimonides, who lived in the 12th century, taught that there are eight degrees of Tzedakah, each one higher than the other. Jewish children often learn

"All men and women belong to one family, the family of Adam and Eve. They all have a claim on each other. Islam teaches us to fulfil the needs of every human being, whether black or white skinned, of any race or any country. Islam also teaches to fulfil the needs of non-Muslims."

*The Children's Book of Islam*

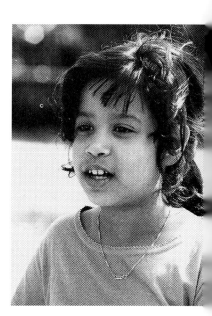

about these eight degrees by making a paper ladder and sticking the phrases (or pictures describing them) on to the steps.

First of all the children should try to work out the order themselves.

Make up sets and working in groups, ask the children to put them in the order that they think is best.

---

Maimonides' order:

The highest degree of Tzedakah:

1  To help by giving a person a job or a loan so that they can support themselves.

2  To give enough, before being asked; you don't know who was given the money and they don't know who gave it.

3  To give enough, before being asked; you know who was given the money but they don't know who gave it.

4  To give enough, before being asked; you don't know who was given the money but they do know who gave it.

5  To give the minimum required, before being asked.

6  To give the minimum required, after being asked.

7  To give too little, but cheerfully.

8  To give too little as if being forced to give.

---

In discussing this list, important values such as responsibility, dignity and humility can be highlighted.

5  Now they know the theory put it into practice. Make contact with local Tzedakah heroes - people in your own community who are helping others - and let them tell you how you can help. Use the children's own enthusiasm, not just for the latest TV appeal but to find out what really concerns them, especially close to home. Raising money should be adventurous, creative, enjoyable and exciting. There many resources to help and if you are stuck, contact Tzedek.

Comment: *In one school a teacher was responding to an enormous number of demands being made on her - to do an effective maths programme, to undertake a Bank of England enterprise project, to implement design and technology, to do a project on money, to get the children through the 11+ etc. Her personal starting point was her values and visions. She wanted the children to be aware of the world in which they live and to contribute to it. She based her work on charity on the parable of the talents (Matthew 25:14-30). Surprising them by giving each child a 'gold' coin, one day she told them the story and then challenged them to use their inner talents to raise money. The children chose to work for street children in Peru. They were completely absorbed in the project, using all their skills of cooperation and communication and their creativity and energy, making note books, food etc. to sell. Needless to say their maths was tackled with fresh vigour as bar charts and pie charts tracked their progress, and design and technology took care of itself.*

*Charity need not be a dreary, patronising affair where we give a little token to those we would rather not think about. Be it termed charity, Tzedakah or Zakat (welfare money for the poor - the third Pillar of Islam), each faith teaches the central importance of giving and of taking action. The way we give is crucial - to give freely and boldly.*

*But the reason why we give is also crucial. Steve Miller expresses the Jewish perspective: "The purpose of these endeavours is to create, bit by bit a more perfect world and thus bring redemption, the messianic age, the Messiah or however you understand it". In Christian terms it is about 'bringing in the kingdom'. And for those of no faith it is perhaps simply about creating a world that works for everyone, a world we want to be part of.*

"Islam stands for brotherhood and social justice. Islam teaches that wealth is a trust from Allah. It should be spent as Allah wants it to be spent. Islam says that the poor and the needy have rights in the wealth of the rich. All good causes have a claim on our wealth."

*The Children's Book of Islam*

**ACTIVITY 4**

# Traffic lights

## What are you doing now?

◊ You might be ending a staff / governor / parent training session on some school policy issue central to the school community, such as equal opportunities or environmental policy.

## You might like to try ⬛ A

You will need a small piece of green, orange and red paper for each person.

1 Each person is given their traffic light set of green, orange and red paper.

2 Reflect on the task in hand. What are the next steps for you individually? What can you do to help implement the policy?

3 First fill in the green sheet, putting on it an action that you can readily take, quite easily in the near future.

4 Secondly fill in the orange sheet, putting on it an action that is more difficult for you.

5 Thirdly - the red sheet - the red light - the one that makes you stop in your tracks. Put on that one the action you know is really hard for you, but which is the action that would make a difference.

6 Share in pairs and then in fours. Take time to talk about the red sheet.

7 In the whole group each person says one thing they will be doing.

8 Review the sheets at the end of term to see if they have changed colour. Has the red become green?

Comment: *This activity enables you to focus on three sorts of action. The red sheet is often the important one. If we are to create something better than we have now, the future will be different and will no doubt require us to do something different from what we have been doing up till now. As long as we go on doing what we have always been doing we will feel relatively comfortable - after all it's familiar. But nothing much will change. To effect change often requires that we move out of our comfort zone. The children asking the shopkeepers to display their posters, the child speaking up at assembly - there are a myriad of risks taken each day by children. Risk, adventure, stepping out, letting go of the familiar, doing what seems impossible, are ingredients of living our values.*

"...the public must learn how to cherish the nobler and rarer plants, and to plant the aloe, able to wait a hundred years for its bloom, or its garden will contain, presently, nothing but potatoes and pot herbs."

*Margaret Fuller*

Marie (aged 10) was doing a project on animals - nice furry ones. In her homework research she came across a book on issues concerning animals and some photos of testing and experimentation on them. Tears welled up. She said nothing but next day went off to school with the book. Her teacher let her use the photocopier and during topic study time Marie and friend set about a cut and paste job designing a poster giving some of the statistics about testing. Some 40 copies of the poster were made. Marie was late home from school that day. She and a friend had visited every shop down the main road and left a poster for display. The last words on the sheet were "Do something!". For several weeks these posters were to be seen in the shops. Meanwhile Marie designed a second poster and with friends organised a community event - an animal rights day raising £145, creating a lot of fun and generating discussion about the issue.

**ACTIVITY 5**

# Strategising

## What are you doing now?

◊  You may be planning to implement a school initiative.

◊  You may be planning to do Tzedakah, raise some money, or undertake some project with your class.

## You might like to try

**1**  Get into pairs, one is A, the other B.  A asks B questions from the Strategising sheet.  A listens actively to B's response and jots down notes.

**2**  Change roles - B questions and A answers.

**3**  Exchange notes and reflect on them.

Comment:  *This example will need to be adapted for use with children to suit the needs of a particular group.*

---

### Some questions to help you strategise

Putting aside all modesty, what have I achieved so far in my work for peace?

How do I make my choices?

What particular strengths do I have?
What particular abilities do I have?
What particular talents do I have?

What have I tried that worked?
What have I tried that didn't work?
What does this teach me?

What circles do I move in?  Who are the people I can most easily reach?
Is this really where I want to be?

What are the major things holding me back?

What is the next challenge for me?

Who will support me?
Who will understand me?
Who will work with me?

Where do I choose to put my energy?  What aspect/s of peace do I want to work on?

What can I do if I get stuck?

In my personal development, is there one thing I could do that would make the rest easier to do?

What goals can I set that are manageable, that will help me get a sense of what I am achieving as time goes by?

What are my next steps?

---

# ACTIVITY 6
# Food is rubbish!

## What are you doing now?

◊   You may be investigating food in science.

◊   You may be considering the effect of litter on the environment in science.

◊   You may be discussing fasting or sacrifice in RE.

## You might like to try C

1   Ask the children to sit quietly for a few moments and to think about all the things they eat and drink during the day, from the moment they get up to the moment they go to bed.  Ask them to think in particular about their favourite foods and drinks.

2   Now ask the children to design an ideal day.  What would they have for breakfast, for a mid-morning snack etc?

3   Ask the children to complete a chart similar to the one below, for their ideal menu, noting down what has to be thrown away in order for them to eat or drink what they have chosen.

| Food/drink | Rubbish | | | | | | | | | |
|---|---|---|---|---|---|---|---|---|---|---|
| | Skin | Pips | Other | Paper | Plastic | Glass | Card | Polystyrene | Aluminium | Other |
| Apple | | | | | | | | | | |
| M&S sandwich | | | | | | | | | | |

4   In pairs, the children share and compare their menus.  What similarities are there?  What differences are there?

**5** As a class, discuss what happens to the rubbish:

   Where is it put?

   What can be burned?

   What happens if it is burned?

   What will rot into the ground?

   What is difficult or impossible to destroy?

**6** Each child now selects one (or more) item/s from her menu which she feels causes problems in terms of rubbish, and makes a commitment not to eat or drink it for a set period, e.g. two weeks. The commitments are shared in the class and recorded. Two weeks later, the class meets again to discuss how things have gone.

**7** Some questions you might like to discuss:

   How did it go?

   How do you feel about what you did?

   How easy/difficult was it to do without the item?

   How will you go on from here?

   Is there anything else you would like to do now?

# ACTIVITY 7
# Letter from the future

## What are you doing now?

◊ You might be looking at the environment in science.

◊ You might be discussing the question of responsibility in RE.

## You might like to try C

**1** Take the children on a guided fantasy to the year 2050 (see Activity 2 in the section on Visioning, page 168).

**2** When they 'return', get into pairs and talk about what they have seen.

**3** Working in small groups, draw a mental map (a chart, diagram or picture) of what they have seen.

**4** In the same groups, work together to compose a letter from the future (2050) to themselves in the present, telling them exactly what they should or should not do now to affect how the world is in the future.

# History of a day [64]

And then, on the stroke of midnight, the people had the world to themselves.  For a long while, so far as we know, they were very quiet.  All through the morning, and all through the afternoon, they just wandered around in small groups - hunting animals with spears and arrows, sheltering in caves, dressing themselves in skins.  At about 6 o'clock in the evening they began to learn about seeds and manure, and so on, and about how to herd and milk animals.  By about half past seven some of them were living in biggish cities.  This was mainly in Egypt and North India and in the countries in between.

Moses came and went at about 8.45.  Buddha in India, Socrates in Greece, Confucius in China all came and went together, though they didn't know each other, at about 10.10.  Christ was at 10.30, as also, give or take a minute or so, were the Great Wall of China and Julius Caesar.  Mahomet was at 11.00.

At around 11.30 there began to be bigger cities in northern Europe.  From about 11.45 onwards people went out from these cities, and they began stealing from the rest of the world.  They stole America, both North and South, they stole northern Asia, they stole India, and just after 11.56 they stole Africa.  At about 11.58 they had a big war amongst themselves, and then had another big war only 50 seconds later.

During the last minute before midnight these people from northern Europe were pushed back out of India and Africa and also back out of many other countries, though not out of North America or northern Asia, where they had become very settled indeed.  Also during this last minute these people invented nuclear weapons, they landed on the moon, they were responsible for almost doubling the world's population, they used up more oil and more metal than had been used in all the previous 23 hours 59 minutes put together.

It was now midnight again.  The start of a new day.

# PART IV

# PERSPECTIVES ON VALUES AND VISIONS

# A Buddhist perspective on Values and Visions

*"There are many thousands of institutions of learning all over the world dedicated to the pursuit of knowledge and the development of the intellect and scientific knowledge, but it is very difficult to find a place of education which is devoted to the cultivation of the heart. Surely this is more important for the quality of our life in our world today."*

This is the comment of Ayya Khema, a widely known Buddhist nun, who has written several books on Buddhism.[65] Her concerns about the development of humanity through Buddhism parallel many of the concerns raised in *Values and Visions* .

In Buddhist thought the word for the mind is 'citta' which means consciousness or the heart and mind together. The purpose of following the Buddhist path is to cultivate skilful or wholesome citta based in wisdom and compassion and to uproot unskilful citta based in greed, hate and delusion. While this process can be seen as a specialised spiritual path, it is also a means of dealing with unhappiness, anxiety and fear in one's daily life and creating positive relationships with family, friends and the environment of the world in which we live. The hope of creating a better world within which to nurture caring and creative relationships is one of the mainsprings of *Values and Visions* and in this respect shares a common aspiration with the Buddhist path. In taking a holistic approach to education by valuing feelings, intuition and imagination as well as the more cognitive faculties, *Values and Visions* is attempting to cultivate the heart in the individual child, the teacher and the community of the school. One of the special feature of *Values and Visions* is that it directly includes the teacher in the learning process by focusing on their spiritual development through the practice of teaching. Another distinguishing feature of *Values and Visions* is the attention given to those aspects of human experience and learning expressed in joy and suffering. In this section which is aimed at 'developing openness to joy and suffering in the classroom and school' both child and teacher are given the opportunity to open up with wisdom towards themselves and compassion to the suffering in the world.

It is necessary to acknowledge the first noble truth in Buddhism before travelling further along the path. This first truth is 'dukka' which is the inherent unsatisfactory nature of life and the suffering in the human condition. The purpose of the teachings or dhamma is to transcend this suffering with the true happiness and freedom of enlightenment. This realisation depends on a recognition of the impermanence of many of the things we cling on to, to bring us happiness. *Values and Visions* is aimed at helping children and teachers find their own values and visions which rest on an understanding and appreciation of the beauty and joy in people and the natural environment rather than the illusory and superficial happiness found in many aspects of contemporary culture.

The three refuges of Buddhism are the Buddha, Dhamma and Sangha. These are the three sources of truth and inspiration for those following this path. The Buddha is the individual who strove to achieve enlightenment through his own efforts and whose search not only gave him a profound understanding of the human condition but insight into all the conditioning factors which had brought him to the point of enlightenment. He represents for Buddhists those personal qualities and experiences which they seek for themselves. So in *Values and Visions* we find a connection with Buddhism in its recognition that the foundation of wisdom and enlightenment is based in self awareness, self understanding and self respect.

The second refuge is the Dhamma, i.e. the teachings, and the means and ways to enlightenment. In *Values and Visions* the means and ways to personal and spiritual development are expressed in 'Key ways' which includes chapters on listening, use of story, reflection, sensory awareness and visioning.

The Sangha is the community in which the path to enlightenment is sustained, preserved and celebrated. It is often stated in the Visuddhimagga [66] that it is essential to be accompanied on the path with good friends who will encourage and support one's efforts. So too in *Values and Visions*, the spiritual growth of individual pupils and teachers is dependent on the community of the school with its commonly shared values and visions.

Veronica Voiels

# A Christian perspective on Values and Visions

The understanding which underlies *Values and Visions* can be seen as clearly (though not exclusively) Christian. However, any exposition of this, while it will touch on very central Christian concepts, should not be taken as a complete statement of these. What follows starts with the fundamental conviction in *Values and Visions* about the spiritual dimension and God, however we understand these, and the four 'key areas': Sense of Self, Sense of Community, Valuing the Earth and Suffering and Joy. It then attempts briefly to show the place that each of these has in Christian understanding.

## God, or Spirit

Christians, like people of other monotheistic faiths, see God as the source of everything: humanity, the earth and the whole cosmos. God is experienced as transcendent - the great mystery above and beyond us, eternal and infinite, not limited by space or time. But God is also experienced as immanent - the one 'in whom we live and move and have our Being'[67] the Spirit of God infuses the whole of creation.

It must be acknowledged, however, that all we try to say about God is inadequate or ambiguous and an inevitably limited attempt to describe the infinite.

This spiritual dimension to our existence, whether described in conventional terms as 'God' or not, underlies the approach of *Values and Visions*.

Christians also believe that in the life, death and resurrection of Jesus, the nature of God as love is most fully shown. Jesus is God incarnate, 'God with us'; he shows us a way through evil and suffering, which is the way of the cross, a path of transforming love. This is celebrated in the Christian rite of the Eucharist, or thanksgiving.

Although the term 'Father' is often used of God, there is a clear strand in the Christian tradition, increasingly emphasised today, which acknowledges feminine as well as masculine aspects of God, and uses both 'Mother' and 'Father' to address God.

## Sense of Self

It is clear in the Bible that men and women are seen as having a spiritual nature, and that there is something of the divine in each individual. Human beings are made 'in the image of God'[68], from whom comes the 'true light which enlightens every one who comes into the world'[69]. Jesus made it clear that human beings in their very nature cannot live on 'bread alone'[70], but depend on the 'word of God' for their essential being. What use will it be, he asks elsewhere, if a person gains the whole world, but loses their life or their 'true self'[71]? This 'true self' will grow when it is oriented towards God.

Because of the need to understand the evil and failure that are part of the human story, and for which human beings seem to have some clear responsibility, there has been much debate in the Christian tradition about the 'fallen nature' of humanity and the need for forgiveness and salvation. However this is precisely understood, the constant falling of human beings, as individuals, communities and nations, into egoism, violence, cruelty, greed and all the evils often called 'sin', has to be recognised. But it should always be seen alongside the amazing human potential for goodness, kindness, generosity, forgiveness and selfless love.

## Sense of Community

Throughout the Bible, the idea of God's covenant with his people is central. This covenant, or sacred agreement, requires that God's people are true to God and act towards their neighbours and towards strangers, with justice and compassion. When they forget the humane laws of the covenant and start exploiting, neglecting or violently oppressing others - when they lose their sense of community - they destroy their relationship with God.

The beliefs that there is the divine in everyone, and that through the incarnation everyone shares a family relationship with God, deepen this emphasis on working for right relationships with all our neighbours. If every individual person is a child of God, sharing God's nature, then all must be given the same dignity and value. And if God has shared our human nature, then that nature has become sacred.

The famous parable of the Sheep and the Goats in St Matthew's Gospel approves of those who cared for their neighbours when hungry, or thirsty, without clothing or shelter, because, however unaware, they were caring for Christ.[72]

It is natural then, that the central Christian tradition has always included a strong awareness of the dependence of human beings on each other, together with active and often costly care for the poor and work for justice and peace.

## Valuing the Earth

In Christian thought, God is the creator of the earth and all it contains - plants, trees, fish, animals. But God is not simply a creator who is separate from what has been made. In particular, the Psalms and the wisdom books speak of the power and beauty of God which pervade nature and reveal God to us.

Human beings are given the fruits of the earth for food, so the relationship of humanity to nature is one of dependence, but the Genesis story makes clear that it is also a relationship of responsibility. Because over the last three hundred years the Church in the west has allowed a fatal separation between spirit and matter, and between sacred and secular, the 'dominion' over nature given to humanity in Genesis has been seen as giving humanity the right to control and exploit nature. The original covenant with nature in Genesis[73] has been largely ignored.

Now, in the late twentieth century, we have become acutely conscious of the destruction caused by the exploitation of the earth, and fearful that our misuse of natural resources will threaten our very survival. So many Christians in the west at present are seeking to recover a proper sense of humility in our relationship with the earth, and an understanding of our responsibility to care for it. There is an increasing emphasis on human dependence on nature and awareness of the spirit of God within nature.

Some visionary passages of the New Testament[74] speak of the tremendous struggle that the whole of the created order is undergoing, and of the 'Cosmic Christ' who will ultimately save and unite the whole of creation.[75]

## Joy and Suffering

The mystery that all religious traditions seek to address is the central human experience of joy and suffering, goodness and evil. Both have to be accepted as part of experience, some meaning grasped, and a creative way through pain and suffering found.

For Christians, that meaning and creative path are to be found in forgiveness and self-giving love that are realised most fully in the life, death and resurrection of Jesus. In this story, the joy is to be found only with the suffering; the two are part of the same reality. Christians are called to follow the same path.

## A final note about *Values and Visions*

True 'spiritual development' is about the whole, about growth in each key area for the child or the school. It is not just about the idea, that is perhaps more usual, of having a relationship with God. For God encompasses and inspires each of the key areas, and the whole, not any part, is the 'spiritual life'.

Barbara Vellacott

# A Hindu perspective on Values and Visions

*In the absence of a member of the Hindu faith on the Values and Visions Development Group, this article has been written by a member of the Development Group who is a lecturer on Multi-faith Education.*

*Values and Visions* as a form of education in personal development and spiritual development has a strong affinity with the Indian religious tradition of Sanatana Dharma, otherwise known as Hinduism. Sanatana Dharma means eternal truth or law, expressed in the symbol ॐ

This symbol is made up of the Sanskrit letters for OM or AUM. It represents the vibration and reverberation of the life-giving energies pervading and sustaining the cosmos which emanates from the ultimate spiritual reality, Brahman. When this same spiritual reality constitutes the true essence of each living being it is called Atman. Thus the central message of the Upanishads [76] is that the essential self (Atman) is identical with the universal soul (Brahman).

*"He (Atman) is myself within the heart, smaller than a grain of rice or a barley corn, or a grain of millet: this is myself within my heart, greater than the earth, greater than the atmosphere, greater than the sky, greater than all these worlds."* [77]

This passage conveys the message that all forms of life are sacred and each aspect of life, human, animal and every part of the natural world is interconnected and interdependent. This important truth begins with a realisation of the nature of the inner self which should be the goal of life.

The affinity with *Values and Visions* lies in the acknowledgement of the importance and value of the inner self and the inner world of the self as a source of inspiration and affirmation. The encouragement given to children to discover their inner selves, and to appreciate and experience the preciousness of life, and to celebrate the beauty and wonder of the natural environment links *Values and Visions* to some of the most fundamental aspirations of the eternal truths of Hinduism.

The 20th century artist and poet, Rabindranath Tagore fulfilled his vision of creating an institution of education in Santaniketan in West Bengal, where the spirit of human nature was nurtured in harmony with the natural environment through the promotion of spirituality through the creative arts. The approaches to learning in *Values and Visions* echoes with the same vibrations which inspired Tagore in his understanding of the real purpose of education.

Veronica Voiels

# A Jewish perspective on Values and Visions

The Jewish tradition is much more focused on what one does, than on what one thinks or believes. The Rabbis (teachers) throughout the ages have concentrated on the questions, 'What does God want of us? What kind of behaviour makes a righteous person?'. Jewish tradition teaches that, 'whether it be Jew or non-Jew, man or woman, free or enslaved - only according to their deeds does the spirit of God rest on them.' (From a 9th century commentary.)

In this spirit the central Jewish values are embodied in the mitzvot or commandments. These range from the mitzvot (singular mitzvah) to observe the Sabbath and Festivals, through to how one should deal in business. All aspects of life are integrated in this framework. Judaism is holistic. Indeed many Jewish people would prefer not to call Judaism just a religion, preferring the term 'a way of life'.

Amongst the mitzvot several are considered to have special value. The mitzvah of education is important because study and understanding leads to righteous action. The mitzvah of tzedakah is the nearest in meaning to charity but its root is the word for justice. In the Jewish tradition giving money to help others is done in order to create a more just world, not just out of a feeling of caring. The rabbis taught that tzedakah must be done with special consideration for the dignity of the recipient, and that the highest form of tzedakah is to work in partnership with someone so that they may become self supporting.

Within Judaism, the key areas of *Values and Visions* - a sense of self, a sense of community, valuing the earth and developing openness to suffering and joy - are central concepts.

God created human beings in his own image. If God is a totally infinite being then each one of us carries that aspect of infinite value. We should learn to respect ourselves and others for this infinite value within us. Each soul is unique. The Hasidic mystical teacher, Rabbi Nachman of Bratslav, taught that this unique soul means that each of us is special, but it also means that we are each alone as there is no other person quite the same as us in the world.

If this applies to individuals, it also applies to communities. Judaism teaches that God started from just one family, Adam and Eve, so that no group of people could later say that they were better than any other. Judaism believes that righteous people of all nations and religions are of equal value. We all have to work together in the world. The Jewish vision of the earth is a cooperative one. In a famous story, a person gets the chance to visit both heaven and hell. They both look the same - a huge room with a table in the middle laden with food. In hell the people are groaning because they have long spoons strapped to their arms. They can reach the food but they cannot bend their arms to get it to their mouths - so they starve for eternity. In heaven all is just the same - the same table, the same spoons - except that here, everyone is content because they have learnt to feed each other.

As well as a sense of the global community the Jewish people have a famously strong sense of their own unique identity and history. All Jewish children learn about the good times and bad times of Jewish history as though they were their own family stories. On a more elevated plane, the discussions and debates that are recorded in Jewish rabbinical books are not just the work of single authors - they are extended conversations between rabbis in different places and spanning many generations all working within the same understanding of what it is to be Jewish. In our liturgy we recite the texts as if we ourselves were the ones who left Egypt in the Exodus and stood at the foot of Mount Sinai to hear the word of God. From this strong sense of ourselves we support the right of all groups to express their own culture.

This Jewish sense of identity has helped to withstand the shocks of many oppressions. Here is not the place to tell at length the sufferings of the Jewish people. Jews were dispersed throughout the world by the Romans, massacred and expelled in Mediaeval times, and suffered the ultimate genocide of the Nazi Holocaust. To some, these experiences may only teach that evil is stronger than good, but to the Jewish people, generation after generation has affirmed that life and good can triumph. Even after the Holocaust the Jewish people have re-affirmed their faith and belief in life.

They are known for enthusiastic celebration, particularly of family events that demonstrate the existence of a new generation. Having suffered so much, the Jew should always be on the side of the oppressed, fighting for justice, ensuring that bystanders cannot just be silent as they were in the 1930s and 1940s.

Perhaps because of its long history, Jewish tradition always thinks long term. The rabbis taught of the importance of planting trees not just for ourselves but for our grandchildren. An awareness of environmental concerns was demonstrated right back to biblical days when fruit trees were forbidden to be cut down even in the midst of wars. Jewish teaching says that God showed creation to Adam and Eve saying, "Do not corrupt and destroy My world, for if you do there will be no one to set it right after you." Yet Jewish teaching is also clear that humanity is the pinnacle of creation. We are stewards of the earth, but the earth is there to serve the needs of people. In modern times both human development and environmental conservation are important.

Judaism does not envisage a static society. Balance is important but so is change. In the Jewish vision the purpose of creation is to bring about the redemption of society. This can be understood in many ways but there is a clear emphasis on the need to work in the world to make it a better place. "Justice, justice shall you pursue" is a central teaching. The repeated theme of the prophets is anger at the failures of governments and individuals to maintain this just society.

But we also have free will - in the Jewish text, to choose good or evil, life or death, blessing or curse. God asks us to "choose life, so that you may live." All is within our hands and so we must take power and not give in. The rabbis of the Talmud also taught that we may feel that the job of changing the world is so huge that even within a generation justice may not prevail, but nevertheless we are not free to give up. We are obliged to work for change.

So the Jewish vision of the world is a passionate, active, assertive, cooperative and diverse one. All of us have a part to play in it.

Note: Judaism does not have a single religious authority. So this description must be seen as one person's interpretation of a rich and pluralist tradition, not as an authoritative text.

Steve Miller

# A Muslim perspective on Values and Visions

Change has always been part of the human condition, but people the world over are now beginning to reject the common assumption that sociopolitical change, usually instigated from remote centres of power, is either natural or necessary for survival. Indeed, usually quite the reverse is the case. It is not synonymous with advancement or progress. It is more the rule than the exception that today this has the effect of destroying a community's social cohesion. It interferes with deep beliefs and long held traditions that have bound people together for centuries. It was through the preservation of this social cohesion, the interdependence of a community's members, the recognisable chain of authority and the closeness to their habitat, that a community was able to survive, rebuild and renew. This required a knowing and a recognition of each other:

*"Oh mankind!*
*We created you from a single pair*
*Male and female*
*And made you into nations and tribes*
*That you may know each other... "*

*Qur'an 49:13*

Knowing is a basis on which to build human relationships and establish understanding. It begins with two people and then radiates out to encompass communities and nations.

The external changes that are inflicted on people today result in the destruction of natural habitats and traditional lifestyles. Complex government systems subject people to upheavals and changes way beyond their understanding and control and have profound, negative effects on their inner cores, resulting in increasing psychosis which is evident today. Perhaps this is why *Values and Visions* is so important. Urban children, particularly, are being progressively disconnected by consumerism from what is natural, from what has been respected as tradition and from their anchors of family and community. The increasing sophistication of material life is accompanied by a corresponding increase in the destitution of the spirit.

In spite of all its advantages, modern urban life has the ability to tear people from their roots through a process we have conveniently termed alienation. For this reason, Muslims try desperately not only to hang on to the family but also to give shape, form and meaning to their lives by recreating the spirit of community.

We humans have survived and thrived on this planet because of our ability to function as a community or a group. Like the more intelligent mammals, i.e. the apes, the elephant and the whale, the young stay with the group for long periods. In keeping with this, the group also has a social organisation which imposes responsibilities on adults to look after the young. It would seem that in the natural patterning of creation there exists a hierarchy of life forms each with its own social organisation and purpose:

*"There is not an animal that lives on the earth*
*Nor a being that flies on its wings*
*But are communities like you..."*

*Qur'an 6:38*

However, the uniqueness of the human community stems from our superior intelligence and our ability to manipulate the environment. That is why we are where we are. Whether we are nomads or city dwellers, we need the group to protect the individual and sustain whatever lifestyles or modes of production or survival mechanisms we have chosen for ourselves.

But there is now conclusive evidence that our very cleverness is our downfall. Community has been sacrificed for technology. The more we bury ourselves in the artifacts of our own creation - cramming more and more into our very brief, selfish lives - the more we distance ourselves from each other and nature. The philosophy of 'progress' as we have now come to define it necessitates the syphoning of the individual from the community, the objective being to place him or her in a competitive process which is intensely destructive. This, as we are now slowly beginning to realise, alienates us from the very community that nurtures us, disconnecting us from the environment that sustains us.

Self hood - which is not the same thing as
individualism - is under threat as the diverse and
long-tested social cohesion that has supported the
inner world of individuals is ripped apart. Alienated
individuals cannot built strong communities. Our
project is to bring back into focus the 'Mizan' - the
balance principle of creation. What better place to
start than the school where for at least a small part
of their lives children can experience the meaning of
community.

Fazlun Khalid

# A non-faith perspective on Values and Visions

*Values and Visions* is for people of all faiths and of no faith. It is not rooted in any one faith tradition although it stems from a Christian background.

*Values and Visions* is about magic, enchantment, wonder and awe. It is about acknowledging our inner self. We are not purely physical creatures with only material needs such as food, water and shelter; we are emotional creatures with spiritual needs such as love, respect and care. We need time to think, to celebrate and to grieve.

*Values and Visions* starts with our own experiences in our relationships with ourselves, others and the earth. These experiences give us joy and suffering: we feel pleasure, confusion, warmth, horror, excitement and fear. These are our everyday experiences, the 'here and now'. The next step is to try and make sense of them. *Values and Visions* offers a variety of ways to do this. By listening to each other we can learn from the experiences of others. By telling our own stories we can begin to make sense of them and inform our own future lives and those of people around us. By being open to the teachings of other traditions we can draw on wisdom both ancient and modern. By taking time and space for reflection and contemplation we can help to clarify our experiences and decide what it is we really want for the future and how we are going to get there. This leads to an increased sense of purpose and a commitment to action. We feel empowered. We feel we can change what we do not like. We can make a difference. We do matter.

Our actions lead us to new experiences, to new feelings of joy and suffering. Again, we can explore these in the ways suggested and identify new or renewed purpose and the action we wish to take, and so the cycle continues...

*Values and Visions* is grounded in the belief that each person is a unique individual of infinite potential. I have potential, therefore I matter. It is about acknowledging our strengths and recognising what each of us has to offer to the community in which we live and the groups of which we are part: family, school, club, neighbourhood, country, world.

*Values and Visions* recognises and builds on our faith in ourselves, in others and in the world around us.

Sally Burns

*Sun Tracks*

*"The Track of the Sun*
*across the Sky*
*Leaves its shining message,*
*Illuminating,*
*Strengthening,*
*Warming,*
*us who are here,*
*showing us we are not alone,*
*we are yet ALIVE!*
*and this fire...*
*Our fire...*
*Shall not die!"*

*Atoni (Choctaw)*
*American Indian Prayers and Poetry*

# A Sikh perspective on Values and Visions

The Sikh community shares many of the values and visions which are implicit in the *Values and Visions* project. In this article we concentrate on those aspects of Sikhism which are concerned with the sense of community and hospitality, spiritual development and the place of suffering and joy in human existence. The article is the result of a long conversation between Roop Singh (of the Sikh Educational Advisory Service, Leeds) and Andrew Burns, coordinator of the *Values and Visions* project.

The main Sikh principles are: Remember God every day. Earn your own living according to your level of skill and ability. Share what you have; this gives great satisfaction and brings joy and happiness.

The concepts of hospitality and sharing underpin the beliefs of the Sikh community. Sikhs value others as themselves, regardless of religion, caste or sex as they are all seen as part of the human race and God resides in every human being; there is the light of God in everyone.

Sikhs give great value to the belief in equal opportunities for all within the community according to people's levels of ability and skills. Men and women equally play a vital part in the life of the Gurdwara (Sikh temple) and the wider community.

The Langar (communal meal) at the Gurdwara is open to all for food and refreshment. It is seen as a blessing to be able to serve and share with other people, preparing and serving food and carrying out the menial tasks such as washing the dishes. This results in the cleansing of oneself, and gives a great sense of contentment and pleasure.

To a Sikh spirituality is recognised as energy, light, life itself, something ticking away inside everyone. Sikhs try to see the value of the faith of others, but remain open to those who feel that the Sikh way of life has something to offer.

Through prayers or meditation the spirit is lifted, one feels contentment and appreciates life. Worshipping in a community creates even more energy. All Sikhs are requested to think of God once a day at the very least. Through daily life the Sikh is required to share or give away what he or she has if required, gaining great satisfaction and spiritual benefit from helping others regardless of who they are and the personal cost involved.

Sikhs believe that the body is a temple and is to be treated with respect. It is not to be abused by eating meat or by the taking of drugs or alcohol. The uncut hair (Keshas) is an outward sign of this respect for the body in its natural form, for the body is an image of the world which is to be treated with care and respect. Sikhs are encouraged to use the natural world with respect and care. The earth, the animals and the environment are to be used only according to need, not greed. The world should be allowed to flourish, looked after by humans who try not to destroy the environment for the sake of it.

Sikhs believe that if you sow the seed, you reap the benefit. Suffering is seen as the result of behaviour in a past life, but rather than concentrating on reincarnation the need is to break the cycle of re-birth and suffering and become one with God by leading a good and useful life in this existence as a human, which is the highest level to be attained on this earth.

Rather than concentrating on the negative those who suffer or who have some disability are encouraged to see how they can contribute positively to the community according to their level of ability.

The Gurus taught that Sikhs had to have very high standards of moral behaviour and were to extend hospitality and protection to all. The uncut hair and the turban means that Sikhs are very visible and easily identified and therefore need to maintain high standards at all times. The faith is basically a very positive one with great emphasis being placed on self discipline and responsibility for one's own actions and for the created world in which we live.

Roop Singh

# A whole school perspective on Values and Visions

*Values and Visions* offers resources and activities that can be utilised throughout the school, at all levels, both in the classroom and in staff and management activities. It is essential that it is seen as being for everyone in the school and that it is firmly embedded in the management ethos of the school. Otherwise there is a risk that the work is reduced to the status of being no more than a good idea on the part of one or more staff, who might leave the school at any time, leaving the work incomplete and with no sound foundation, under which circumstances it is likely to wither and die away.

One of the main aims of the project is that the school will be working together as a whole school, developing its school ethos through a focus on shared *Values and Visions*. This has important implications for the school and its management.

The whole school, head, teachers, non-teaching staff, pupils and governors will need to establish a clear, shared understanding of their own values and visions. The handbook will provide schools with the resources and processes to undertake this task, but the values and visions will be those of the school and will not be provided by some external source.

It is important that everyone is involved in the process. Many schools have detailed policies on all aspects of the school ethos but omit to share them, and the necessary training, with lunch-time organisers and other non-teaching staff. Parents and governors also need to be drawn into the process if we are to establish a strong sense of community together.

The work undertaken by staff and children must be seen to be valued by senior staff and governors through active participation, enthusiasm, use of staff time and resources being committed to the work.

It is vital that the school sets itself reasonable goals for this work, maintaining progress and momentum without contributing to excessive stress levels for all those involved.

Everyone needs to be clear as to what it is the school is trying to address, grounded in the 'here and now' of the particular school rather than in some hypothetical ideal world that might or might not be desirable in the future.

One school saw this as an opportunity to consider the situation facing staff and children at break times; others have looked at listening as an issue, whilst introducing the work on contemplation and reflection was the starting point for another school.

It is not practical or desirable for schools to tackle all aspects of school ethos suggested by the work in the handbook. The school will need some sense of clarity and unity on how it wants to work on spiritual and moral development and a sense of community. Many of the activities in the handbook enable staff to work together to achieve this clarity. This may be an unusual experience for some staff but it is a vital part of the process, and therefore needs to be tackled with sensitivity and forethought.

We are not suggesting that schools are driven to go through this process by the spectre of an OFSTED/OHMCI (Wales) inspection - the work is of great value to any school whatever the circumstances. However, *Values and Visions* has a structure to offer a school considering its readiness for inspection and is a visible sign to inspectors that a school is attempting to address important issues and has embarked on the journey to explore the ethos which is most desirable for the individual school. OFSTED inspectors have indicated their belief that *Values and Visions* has a lot to offer schools.

Using this handbook offers the school a chance to create an environment where values can be articulated and visions clarified, in order to build schools - and a world - in which people matter.

Andrew Burns

# NOTES

1   The Third General Assembly of the Ecumenical Association of Third World Theologians, January 1992.

2   Statement on the Justice, Peace and Integrity of Creation Process from the World Council of Churches, Basel 1989.

3   This is now also called the 'Two-Thirds World' as this is the proportion of the human population that lives there.

4   Jon Sobrino in the Pope Paul VI lecture, March 1992.

5   This refers to the experience of working on World Studies and Values and Visions with some 1600 teachers, heads and students in the Greater Manchester area between 1982 and 1992.

6   Those whose ancestors were the original inhabitants of their lands, since colonised by foreigners.

7   The Prophetic Imagination, Walter Brueggemann (see bibliography).

8   Adapted from a piece of work by Patrick Whitaker.

9   Useful resources for this activity are Behind the Scenes, Birmingham DEC, and Living and Learning in a Tanzanian Village, Manchester DEP. Numerous photopacks are available from development education centres; see the address list.

10  By the term 'South' we are referring to what is often called the 'Third World'. Many think that the latter term marginalises what is in fact the majority world.

11  We are indebted to Sharing Nature with Children (see bibliography) for the activities: Heartbeat of a tree, Sounds, Micro-hike, Webbing, Earth windows.

12  Adapted from an idea in First Focus (see bibliography).

13  We have drawn from the fuller and richer version of this earth walk which can be found in Making Global Connections (see bibliography - Suffering & Joy).

14  This story comes from Hope for the Earth by Christian Aid, a leaflet produced for Harvest 1988 (see bibliography). There are numerous other excellent free leaflets on this theme from Christian Aid (see address list).

15  Many individuals and organisations, including the World Council of Churches, have researched and written about this suffering. Albert Nolan, in his book, Jesus before Christianity, (Darton, Longman and Todd), writes: "At present something like 2,000 million people (nearly two-thirds of the human race) live in subhuman conditions with insufficient food, clothing and shelter. Hundreds of millions of people are born into this world to experience little more than the pangs of hunger and sufferings which result from malnutrition and deprivation. Only God knows how many millions die of starvation. Our present situation has become too horrible to contemplate - let alone the future."

16  The Great Wave 1492-1992 (see bibliography) offers an alternative history of encounter and resistance in the Caribbean.

17  This is taken from Don't Just Do Something, Sit There (see bibliography - Stillness & Contemplation). This is a valuable resource for developing children's spiritual awareness.

18  Care needs to be taken in choosing images. The head who devised this activity originally suggested an image of war but then decided this raised just too many questions. The aid agencies have produced numerous photopacks which would be of use, or you might use an image from the newspaper. In choosing photos from the South (or so-called 'Third World') it is important to ensure that any negative images are balanced by positive images of people living their lives. The media often promote pathological images that encourage a patronising and racist attitude.

19  This activity is taken from a Christian Aid resource for Harvest 1985. These resources are produced regularly and can be obtained free from Christian Aid or from DEP (see the address list).

20  The vast majority of farmers in the world are in fact women. Whilst they rarely own the land it is the women who work the land in two thirds of the world.

21 This story is taken from the Christian Aid pack Eritrea: Africa's Newest Country.

22 This piece of work is based on a Christian Aid resource Good news for a Change (Christian Aid week 1986) and adapted by John Roussel, Christian Aid, Manchester, UK.

23 'Southern Voices' has undertaken specific work to enable effective contact and encounters between people from the South (or so-called 'Third World') and school teachers in Manchester, UK (see the address list).

24 See Murder in the Playground and Racism in Schools: new research evidence (see bibliography).

25 This is a simplified version of Rafa Rafa (see bibliography).

26 Simulation Game experienced by the author at the 1989 TEAL (Teaching English as an Additional Language) conference in Canada - source unknown.

27 The Coffee Chain Game is a 12 page booklet, published by Oxfam in 1994 (see bibliography). It contains background information and activities suitable for children aged 14 and over, together with ideas for action and suggested resources. We reproduce here a much simplified version.

28 Spanner in the Works is a useful source (see bibliography - Encounter).

29 Sunship Earth by Steve van Matre (see bibliography).

30 By 'listening to self' we mean times of stillness, reflection, meditation and prayer.

31 The best resource for structured discussion is still Debate and Discussion (see bibliography).

32 Listening to scripture is inherent to all this work on spiritual development. Within each faith there are teachings which are needed for our world today. Hearing the teaching will involve being open to listening.

33 Innovatory circle work has been undertaken by Geoffrey Court and colleagues in Tower Hamlets, London (see useful addresses).

34 Although the idea may have its roots in Native American tradition, the term 'Magic Spot' is part of the 'Earthkeepers' Earth Education programme devised by the Institute for Earth

Education, Box 288, Warronville, Illinois 60555, USA.

35 Adapted from Making RE More Effective (see bibliography).

36 Taken from the Christian Aid leaflet, A World Together.

37 Abridged from a story by Annabel Williams-Ellis (see bibliography).

38 A national survey in autumn 1992 found that 93 percent of adults in England find their lives to be intolerably stressful.

39 Pax Christi and Christian Aid have produced materials which specifically address this.

40 Christian Aid is a good source of up-to-date stories about positive change in the world.

41 The science lesson with the hoop (see the section on Earth on page 39), illustrates how science can be the time for delight, insight and celebration.

42 "And the Lord said 'Listen to my words. If he were your prophet and nothing more, I would make myself known to him in a vision, I would speak with him in a dream. But my servant Moses is not such a prophet; of all my household he alone is faithful. With him I speak face to face, openly and not in riddles'." Numbers 12: 6-8.

43 See the section on Stillness and Contemplation, page 129, for ideas on relaxing and focusing, and also Mary Stone's Don't Just Do Something, Sit There.

44 'Peace' has many facets and it would be misleading to imagine it simply as calm or the absence of noise and war. Brian Wren's poem evokes a rich concept of peace. The full text to the poem can be found in Bread of Tomorrow (see bibliography).

45 The Great Wave (see bibliography).

46 The best description of mental maps is in the classic Learning for Change by Robin Richardson. At the moment this is unfortunately out of print. Copies may be available from Development Education Centres.

47 The Management for Change project based at Manchester Development Education Project worked on the issue of how to sustain policy

and structures which support the process of change in schools. *The School is Us* (see bibliography).

48 Under the national curriculum equal opportunities is a legal requirement.

49 There is at present enough for all. The difficulty is one of distribution and sharing. This is covered well in the section, *Food Comes First* in *Making Global Connections* (see bibliography).

50 See Cathie Holden, *Teaching About the Future with Younger Children* in *Studying the Future* (see bibliography - Suffering & Joy).

51 *The Guardian*, 20.10.92, 'Escape from the culture class'.

52 See the section on Community, page 21, where a guided fantasy is used to explore an ideal school. Invariably teachers come up with things that are very possible.

53 See the section on Purpose and Action, page 181.

54 As in all this work there must be sensitivity. There may well be children in your class who are travellers. Others will be homeless, or are having their home repossessed, or have very inadequate housing.

55 *Doorways* by the Save the Children Fund has a good selection of photos.

56 *A Place to Call My Own* by Linnea Renton, a pack available from Crisis and DEP, is a secondary resource but is a mine of information and ideas that could be adapted for other ages. See address list.

57 The pack, *Homes* brings in a valuable travellers' perspective. See bibliography: Suffering & Joy.

58 Information about these from Crisis as above.

59 See *Use Both Sides of Your Brain* (see bibliography).

60 This is an abridged version of Joanna Macy's meditation on the Web of Life in *Despair and Empowerment*. In *Integral Spirituality*, Donal Dorr adapts this same meditation to focus on God's providence in creating us.

61 *Tzedek: A Study Anthology* (see bibliography). Tzedek is also the name of a Jewish body involved in social action globally. See address list.

62 A ranking exercise might help here: *Introductory Manual on Peace Education* (see bibliography - Community).

63 Adapted from *The Book of Miracles* (see bibliography).

64 From *Global Teacher, Global Learner* (see bibliography).

65 *Being nobody, going nowhere. Meditations on the Buddhist path* (see bibliography).

*When the Iron Eagle Flies. Buddhism for the West* (see bibliography).

66 *The Path of Purification. Visuddhimagga* (see bibliography).

67 Acts 17:28.

68 Genesis 1:26.

69 John 1:9.

70 Matthew 4:4.

71 Matthew 16:26.

72 Matthew 25:31-46.

73 Genesis 9.

74 Romans 8:18-23.

75 Ephesians 1:9-10.

76 The Upanishads are part of the Vedas which ard the sacred books of the Indian religious tradition.

77 Chandogya Upanishad, Book III, 14:3-5. From *Hindu Scriptures* (see bibliography).

# BIBLIOGRAPHY

# Key Areas

## SELF

Borba, M., & Borba, D. (1982). Self esteem (Volumes 1 & 2). San Francisco: Harper Collins.

Prutzman, P., Stern, L., Burger, M. L., & Bodenhammer, G. (1988). Friendly classroom for a small planet: Children's creative response to conflict program. Philadelphia: New Society Publishers.

Save the Children Fund & UNICEF (1990). Rights of the child topic books (set of four books). London: SCF/UNICEF.

Walker, D. (1990). Gender equality: An effective resource for today's classroom. Wisbech: Learning Development Aids.

Wichert, S. (1989). Keeping the peace: Practising cooperation and conflict resolution with preschoolers. Philadelphia: New Society Publishers. OP.

## COMMUNITY

Brueggemann, W. (1978). The prophetic imagination. London: S.C.M. Press Ltd. OP.

Dodgson, R., & Midwinter, C. (1992). Living and learning in a Tanzanian village: A child's perspective. Manchester: Development Education Project.

Gregory, R. (Ed.) (1985). Exploring a theme: Communities. London: Christian Education Movement. OP.

Isaacson, G., & Lamont, G.. Introductory manual on peace education. Manchester: Development Education Project.

Leeds City Council (1992). Say no to bullying. Leeds: Leeds City Council, Department of Education.

Maidenhead Teachers' Centre (1987). Doing things in and about the home. Stoke-on-Trent: Trentham Books.

Masheder, M. (1991). Let's cooperate. London: Peace Pledge Union.

Peck, M. S. (1990). The different drum. London: Arrow Books.

Thomas, P. et al. Getting on with others. London: The Woodcraft Folk.

## EARTH

Brandling, R. (1984). First focus: A collection of stories for assembly. London: Bell & Hyman.

CAFOD. Renewing the earth: Study guide for groups. London: CAFOD.

Christian Aid (1988). Going, going, gone: Activities about the rainforest. London: Christian Aid.

Christian Aid (1990). Handle with care: A teacher resource pack exploring a Christian response to development and the environment. London: Christian Aid.

Cornell, J. B. (1989). Sharing nature with children. Watford: Exley Publications Ltd. Version activities taken from (footnote 10) and copyright obtained from Exley. OP. See below.

Cornell, J. B. (1994). Sharing nature with children. London: Deep Books Ltd.

DEC. Birmingham et al. (1992). It's our world too: A local-global approach to environmental education at key stages 2 and 3. Birmingham: Development Education Centre and South Yorkshire Development Education Centre.

Lyle, S., & Roberts, M. (1988). Arctic child. Maenllwyd, Camarthen: Green Light Publications.

Lyle, S., & Roberts, M. (1988). Rainforest child. Maenllwyd, Camarthen: Green Light Publications.

Masheder, M. (1994). Let's enjoy nature. London: Green Print.

Masheder, M. (1995). Windows to nature. London: WWF UK.

Palmer, M. (1995). Worlds of difference. Oxford: Blackie.

Palmer, M., Nash, A., & Hattingh, I. (Eds.) (1987). Faith and nature. Godalming, Surrey: Rider. OP.

Parker, M. (1990). The living churchyard. London: Community Service Volunteers.

Randle, D. (1991). Teaching green. London: Green Print.

Van Matre, S. (1989). Sunship earth. Institute of Earth Education.

Wilson, R. (1988). Starting from a walk. Stoke-on-Trent: Trentham Books.

## SUFFERING & JOY

Althea (1988). When Uncle Bob died. Cambridge: Dinosaur Publications.

Birmingham DEC. Water. Birmingham: Development Education Centre.

Bridle, M., Barnfield, J., & Stone, M. (1990). Fala Favela: Photographs and activities on shantytown life in Brazil. London: CAFOD, CCODP, CIIR, CRS, SCIAF, MDDDF Brazil and Trocaire.

CAFOD, Christian Aid, Oxfam, Save the Children Fund. (1992). The great wave: 1492-1992. London: CAFOD, Christian Aid, Save the Children Fund, Oxfam.

Christian Aid (1982). The Trading game. London: Christian Aid.

Christian Aid (1985). There's enough. London: Christian Aid.

Christian Aid (1982). The World feast game. London: Christian Aid.

Fisher, S., & Hicks, D. (1985). World studies 8-13. Harlow: Oliver & Boyd. OP.

Greig, S. (1992). New faces, new places: Changusu is going back home/ All about our camp/ Amal's story/ Isha's story. London: Save the Children Fund.

Hicks, D., & Steiner, M. (1989). Making global connections. Harlow: Oliver & Boyd.

Morley, J. (1992). Bread of tomorrow. London: SPCK and Christian Aid.

Najda, R., & Reid, P. (1991). Homes: An active learning pack for 6-12 year olds. London: Save the Children Fund & Scottish Development Education Centre.

Oxfam. (1993). How does the world look to you? An activity pack on the use and interpretation of images. Oxford: Oxfam Publications.

Taylor, B. (1992). Doorways. London: Save the Children Fund.

# Key Ways

## ENCOUNTER

Brown, C., Barnfield, J., & Stone, M. (1990). Spanner in the works: Education for racial equality and social justice in white schools. Stoke-on-Trent: Trentham Books.

Hopkins, S., & Winters, J. (1990). Discover the world: Empowering children to value themselves, others and the earth. Philadelphia: New Society Publishers.

Kelly, E. & Cohn, T. (Eds.) (1988). Racism in schools: new research evidence. Stoke-on-Trent: Trentham Books.

Masheder, M. (1989). Let's play together: Over 300 co-operative games for children and adults. London: Green Print.

McDonald, I. et al. (1989). Murder in the playground: The Burnage report. London: Longsight Press.

Oxfam. (1994). Coffee chain game. Oxford: Oxfam Publications.

Ross, C., & Ryan, A. (1991). Can I stay in today, Miss? Improving the school playground. Stoke-on-Trent: Trentham Books.

## LISTENING

Hope, A., & Timmel, S. (1984). Training for transformation. Zimbabwe: Mambo Press.

Richardson, R. Debate and decision. Out of print but a few copies are available from DEP Manchester.

## STILLNESS & CONTEMPLATION

Beesley, M. (1990). Stilling: A pathway for spiritual learning in the national curriculum. Salisbury: Diocesan Board of Education.

De Mello, A. (1983). Wellsprings: A book of spiritual exercises. New York: Doubleday.

De Mello, A. (1988). Sadhana: A way to God. Gujerat, India: Anand. OP.

Fugitt, E. D. (1983). "He hit me back first!" Creative visualization activities for parenting and teaching - Self esteem through self-discipline. Rolling Hills Estates, California: Jaalmar Press.

Stone, M. K. (1992). Don't just do something, sit there: Developing children's spiritual awareness. Lancaster: St. Martin's College Primary R.E. Team.

Tewari, G. N. (1986). Yogabhyasa: Learn & practice (Parts 1-5). New Delhi: Pitambar Publishing Company.

## CELEBRATION & GRIEVING

Byars, B. (1993). Good-bye chicken little. London: Heinemann Educational.

CAFOD, Christian Aid, SCIAF and Trocaire (1992). A generous land: Words and pictures for prayer and reflection from Latin America and the Caribbean. London: CAFOD, Christian Aid, SCIAF and Trocaire.

Morris, L. & Perkins, G. (1991). Remembering mum. London: A. & C. Black.

Sanders, P. (1990). Death and dying. London: Gloucester Press.

Snell, N. (1989). Emma's cat dies. London: Evans Brothers - Books for Children.

Ward, B. (1993). Healing grief: A guide to loss and bereavement. London: Century Vermilion.

West, S. (1991). The magic of pleasant discoveries: Autumn. Brighton: Open-sez-me.

West, S. (1991). The magic of pleasant discoveries: Spring. Brighton: Open-sez-me.

West, S. (1991). The magic of pleasant discoveries: Summer. Brighton: Open-sez-me.

West, S. (1991). The magic of pleasant discoveries: Winter. Brighton: Open-sez-me.

An extensive booklist on children and bereavement can be obtained from:

Cruse - Bereavement Care, 126 Sheen Road, Richmond, Surrey, TW9 1UR.

## SENSORY AWARENESS

Bourne, M. J. et al. (1988). Fruits and vegetables of the Caribbean. London: Macmillan.

Chan, M. et al. (1990). Fruits project pack. London: Mantra Publishing.

Exley, H. (Ed.) (1995). What it's like to be me. Watford: Exley Publications Ltd.

## STORY

Birmingham DEC. (1991). Start with a story: Supporting young children's exploration of issues. Birmingham: Development Education Project.

Brody, E. et al. (Eds.) (1992). Spinning tales, weaving hope: Stories of peace, justice and the environment. Philadelphia: New Society Press.

De Mello, A. (1982). The song of the bird. New York: Doubleday.

Garvie, E. (1989). Story as vehicle. Bristol: Multilingual Matters.

Hammond, J. et al. (1991). New methods in R.E. teaching: An experiential approach. Harlow: Oliver & Boyd.

Ikeda, D. (1991). The cherry tree. Oxford: Oxford University Press.

Mellor, B. et al. (1984). Making stories. London: ILEA English Centre.

Mellor, B. et al. (1984). Changing stories. London: ILEA English Centre.

Naidoo, B. (1995). Journey to Jo'burg: A South African story. London: Longman Education.

Rushdie, S. (1993). Haroun and the sea of stories. London: Puffin.

Williams-Ellis, A. (1981). Tales from the Far East, Africa and the Caribbean. Heinemann Ltd.

Wood, A., & Richardson, R. (1993). Inside stories: Wisdom and hope for changing worlds. Stoke-on-Trent: Trentham Books.

## VISIONING

Buzan, T. (1976). Use both sides of your brain. London: Dutton & Co.

Dorr, D. (1990). Integral spirituality: Resources for community, justice, peace and the earth. Ireland: Gill and Macmillan.

Hall, E. et al. (1990). Scripted fantasy in the classroom. London: Routledge.

Hicks, D. (1991). Exploring alternative futures: A teacher's interim guide. London: Institute of Education, Global futures project.

Hicks, D. (Ed.) (1994). Preparing the future: Notes and queries for concerned educators. USA.: Adamtine Press.

Holden, C. Teaching about the future with younger children. Ch 2 in Slaughter. R. (Ed). 1989. Studying the future: An introductory reader. Commission for the Future, Australian Bicentennial Authority.

Macy, J. (1983). Despair and personal power in the nuclear age. Philadelphia: New Society Publishers. 1983.

Murdock, M. (1987). Spinning inward: Using guided imagery with children for learning, creativity and relaxation. Boston and London: Shambala. OP.

Renton, L. (1993). A place to call my own. London: Crisis.

Slaughter, R. (1989). Studying the future: An introductory reader. Commission for the Future and Australian Bicentennial Authority.

## PURPOSE & ACTION

Aspinall, R. (1988). Creactivity: Creative workshops for world concern. London: YCare International.

Miller, S. Tzedek: Study anthology. London: Tzedek.

# Other useful resources

Bakar, A. S. et al. (1992). Playing in harmony: An early years resource pack. Scotland: Save the Children Fund.

Birmingham DEC. (1991). Why on earth? An approach to science with a global dimension at key stage 2. Birmingham: Development Education Centre.

CAFOD (1992). Esperanza: Aspects of Latin America. London: CAFOD.

CAFOD (1992). Shantytown kids: A partnership pack for primary schools on Brazil. London: CAFOD.

Chapman, J. et al. (1990). Rights of the child (set): The whole child/ It's our right/ Keep us safe/ Teacher's handbook. London: Save the Children.

Conroy, E. K., & Regan, C. (1992). Food matters. Birmingham: Development Education Centre and Trocaire.

Cox, K., & Hughes, P. (1993). Oxford infant history: Big book. Oxford: Oxford University Press.

Ellis, V. F. (1990). First book about Africa. Orange, New Jersey: Just Us Books Inc.

Epstein, D., & Sealey, A. (1990). "Where it really matters": Developing anti-racist education in predominantly white primary schools. Birmingham: Development Education Centre.

Fell, G. (1992). "You're only a dinner lady." A training pack for lunchtime organisers in primary schools. Manchester: Strategies for a less violent environment.

Green, R. L. (Ed.) (1989). A salute to historic black firsts. Chicago: Empack.

Green, R. L. (Ed.) (1989). A salute to historic blacks in the arts. Chicago: Empack.

Igus, T. (Ed.). (1992). Book of black heroes: Great women in the struggle. Orange, New Jersey: Just Us Books Inc.

Khema, A. (1987). Being nobody, going nowhere. Meditations on the Buddhist path. Boston, USA: Wisdom Books.

Khema, A. (1991). When the iron eagle flies. Buddhism for the West. London: Penguin Books.

McDonnagh, S. SSC, (1990). The greening of the church. London: Orbis Books.

McFarlane, C. (1991). Themework: A global perspective in the primary curriculum in the 90's. Birmingham: Development Education Centre.

Nanamoli, B. (trans.) (1991). The path of purification. Visuddhimagga. Buddhist Publication Society.

Northampton County Council (1989). Primary images. Northampton: County Council, Education Department.

Renton, L. (1993). The school is us. Manchester: Development Education Project.

Rieser, R. et al. (1992). Disability equality in the classroom: A human rights issue. London: Disability Equality in Education.

Roman Catholic Bishops conference of England and Wales. Curriculum Guidance: A commentary for Catholic schools.

Scottish Catholic International Aid Fund. The water of life. Glasgow: Scottish Catholic International Aid Fund.

Steiner, M. (1994). Learning from experience: World studies in the primary curriculum. Stoke-on-Trent: Trentham Books.

Sullivan, D., & Gallagher, J. (1988). R.E. The primary years: Promise and potential for the way ahead. London: Harper Collins.

Zaehner, R.C. (trans.) 1989. Hindu Scriptures. Dent.

If any of the above titles are unavailable you may be able to borrow them from your local library or Development Education Centre. Contact Manchester Development Education Project for details.

# Quotations source list

A range of writers are quoted in the text. This list contains sources where possible.

Exley, H. (Ed.) (1995). What it's like to be me. Watford: Exley Publications.

Brady, H. The Living Arctic. Faber & Faber.

Burger, J. Gaia Atlas of First Peoples. (1990). London: Gaia Books Ltd.

De Mello, A. One minute wisdom. New York: Doubleday.

Hasbudak, Z., and Simons, B. Zeynep: That really happened to me. ALTARF.

Hicks, D., & Steiner, M. (1989). Making global connections. Harlow: Oliver & Boyd.

Hope, A., & Timmel, S. (1984). Training for transformation. Zimbabwe: Mambo Press.

Islamic Foundation (1979). The children's book of Islam (Vol. 2). Leicester: The Islamic Foundation.

Jackson, R., & Killingley, D. (1991). Moral issues in the Hindu tradition. Stoke-on-Trent: Trentham Books.

Kayani, M. S. (1985). Love all creatures. Leicester: The Islamic Foundation.

Lopez, B. Arctic Dreams. (1987).

Luling, V. (1984). Aborigines. London: Macdonald & Co.

Morley, J. (1992). Bread of tomorrow. London: SPCK and Christian Aid.

Norberg-Hodge, H. Ancient Futures: Learning from Ladakh. Rider Books.

Northampton County Council (1989). Primary images. Northampton: County Council, Education Department.

Notes from Positive Indian Parenting Programme run in Victoria, Canada (1989).

Partnov, E. (1982). The quotable woman. New York: Facts on File Inc.

Pepper, M. (Ed.) (1989). A Dictionary of religious quotations. London: Andre Deutsch.

Revised English Bible (1989). Oxford: Oxford and Cambridge University Presses.

Schiller, D. (1994). The Little Zen Companion. Workman Publishing Company.

Sharpe, J. E. (1987). American Indian prayers and poetry. Cherokee Indian Reservation: Cherokee Communications.

Taylor, A. (1984). Sharing. London: Girl Guides Association.

Taylor, A. (1985). Searching. London: Girl Guides Association.

# Images source list

Hanns-Jorg Anders/Ridge Press: p 151.

Kerry Brown: pp 9, 41, 167.

Sally Burns: p 146.

Garry Clarke, Copyright: pp xii, xv, xxii, 3, 5, 11, 12, 13, 20, 21, 34, 36, 42, 46, 56, 59, 63, 75, 83, 86, 91, 97, 101, 107, 120, 122, 135, 136, 142, 148, 164, 177, 185, 187, 189.

Rick Dodgson/DEP: pp 17, 33, 61, 127, 195.

Sally and Richard Greenhill/Birmingham DEC: p109.

Jenny Harrison/Children in Focus: 'Baby Rosa' p 14; 'Hanuka' p 161.

Wolfgang Kaehler/UNICEF: p 165.

Eileen Langsley/Wildcat Cards: p 123.

Martin Leach/Christian Aid: p 72.

Tina Manley/UNICEF: p 159.

Jeni McKenzie/Children in Focus: 'Cuddling' p57; 'Can You Taste the Difference?' p 137.

Maggie Murray/Format: p 67.

Piper Hill Special School: p 39.

Petra Rohr-Rouendaal: Zebras p 32.

Rajendra Shaw/Christian Aid: p 74.

Susie Renear: p 178.

Lizzie Slatter: pp 47, 113, 129, 131, 134, 143.

Paula Solloway/Leeds Postcards: p 79.

Deborah Thompson: pp xix, 23, 99, 181.

Paul Weinberg/Leeds Postcards: p 115.

# USEFUL ADDRESSES

**For details of trainers, training opportunities and resources, contact:**

**Manchester Development Education Project**
**c/o Manchester Metropolitan University**
**801 Wilmslow Road**
**Didsbury**
**Manchester**
**M20 2QR**
**0161 445 2495**

To find out where your nearest Development Education Centre is, contact:

Development Education Association (DEA)
29-31 Cowper Street
London
EC2A 4AP
0171 490 8108

Other useful addresses:

CAFOD
2 Romero Close
London
SW9 9TY
0171 733 7900

Christian Aid
PO Box 100
London
SE1 7RT
0171 620 4444

The Circle Works
2 Medway Buildings
Medway Road
Bow
London
E3 5DR
0181 983 3967

The Council of Christians and Jews
1 Dennington Park Road
London
NW6 1AX
0171 794 8178

Crisis
7 Whitechapel Road
London
E1 1DU
0171 377 0489

International Sacred Literature Trust
23 Darley Avenue
Manchester
M20 2ZD
0161 445 2523

Islamic Foundation for Ecology and Environmental Science
57 Brecon Road
Handsworth
Birmingham
B20 3RW
0121 523 4264

The Jewish Representative Council of Greater Manchester and Region
Jewish Cultural Centre
Bury Old Road
Manchester
M8 6FY
0161 720 8721

Oxfam
274 Banbury Road
Oxford
OX2 7DZ
01865 311311

Sikh Educational Advisory Services
9 Woodland Grove
Leeds
LS7 4HJ
0113 260 2484

Southern Voices
St Peter's House
Precinct Centre
Oxford Road
Manchester
M13 9GH
0161 273 2228

Tzedek
26 Goodwin Vale
London
N10 2HA
0181 883 7453

UNICEF UK
55 Lincoln's Inn Fields
London
WC2A 3NB
0171 405 5592

The World Council of Churches
Rte de Ferney 150
1211 Geneva
Switzerland
00 4122 791 6111

The World Studies Project
c/o Manchester Metropolitan University
799 Wilmslow Road
Didsbury
Manchester
M20 2QT
0161 247 2316